Leadership and Oversight

Leadership and Oversight

NEW MODELS FOR EPISCOPAL MINISTRY

Malcolm Grundy

mowbray

Published by Mowbray
A Continuum Imprint

The Tower Building	80 Maiden Lane
11 York Road	Suite 704
London	New York
SE1 7NX	NY 10038

www.continuumbooks.com

First published 2011

British Library Cataloguing-in-Publication Data
A catalogue record for this book is available from the British Library.

ISBN: PB: 978–1–4411–4401–0

Typeset by Fakenham Photosetting Ltd, Fakenham, Norfolk
Printed and bound in Great Britain by the MPG Books Group

CONTENTS

ACKNOWLEDGEMENTS

It would not have been possible to produce this book without the immense contribution made by those I discuss these issues with in the many seminars and meetings that continue to fill my life. Without the opinions and experience of clergy, paid and unpaid, and lay people of all kinds my ideas would not have been stimulated and then sharpened. I hope that many friends and colleagues will see their concerns expressed and explored here. In my life as a consultant and mentor it has been the greatest privilege to be able to share in the experiences of many senior leaders. I am grateful to have the knowledge given by so many confidences. The frustrations about life in the church shared with me by senior leaders have energized and confirmed my determination to develop the perhaps rather too strident ideas and opinions contained in some parts of this book.

In particular members of staff at York St John University, in the city where I live, have been of the greatest help and encouragement. Professor Sebastian Kim has encouraged and ordered my thoughts on numerous occasions. The Rev Dr Andrew Village has been rigorous in getting me to clarify the questions I need to ask. The Rev Dr Gary Wilton, while at York and subsequently as the Church of England's representative to the European Union first felt that I should reflect in this way using the experiences of my own ministry as a springboard.

It is a great privilege to have a preface contributed by The Rt Rev John Pritchard, Bishop of Oxford. I am also indebted to Bishop Lars-Göran Lönnermark, former Bishop of Skara, for research information about life and work in the Church of Sweden. By appointing me as their first Director, the Trustees of the Foundation for Church Leadership enabled me to enter into the concerns of senior church leaders in a very privileged way. I will always be grateful to them.

It has been a great joy to have had the encouragement of the editorial team at Continuum from the time when this book began as an idea in my mind to its professionally guided publication. There will be inaccuracies and probable distortions in some parts of this book and for all of these I take sole responsibility.

Malcolm Grundy
Michaelmas 2010

PREFACE

The deep public divisions in episcopal churches are there for all to see. In this book the reasons for those divisions are analyzed in some detail. Ways to resolve this all-consuming situation are essential for the members, clergy and leaders of those churches. This book begins with a description of the many places where episcopal churches have become dysfunctional. It then sets out to bring into the centre of 'the memory' of these churches that they are episcopal which means that their reason for existence is to give and receive oversight in a mutually beneficial way.

In order that such oversight can be owned by all those concerned, the history of the development of episcopally led churches is traced as are the appointment methods in some of the principal western episcopal churches. Ecumenical agreements regarding the centrality of episcopacy in the leadership and oversight of many denominations strengthen the argument for rediscovering the memory of this, the earliest form of church organization.

Understandings and expectations of leadership and networked oversight from within and outside the churches is charted and analyzed. Significant, clear and accessible models for the future governance of episcopal churches emerge from these detailed descriptions. The method adopted in each chapter is one of studied theological, historical and political mapping which lead to strident conclusions followed by practical descriptions of ways forward.

This is a book which dwells on one subject solely in order to offer a new understanding of what it is which can give an underlying unity to episcopally led churches. Those in these churches who can assent to a renewed and developed understanding of leadership and oversight can address their differences from a common understanding and starting-point. Others who represent division and difference will be challenged about their motivation and their understanding of the nature of the church within which they have accepted the call to be a leader.

Church leaders and congregations with their clergy are invited to share in a journey. It is one which will bring a renewed commitment to a church which through the centuries has been loyal to its heritage and story. Again and again it has been able to renew itself in the service of the Gospel. The challenges facing today's church and its leaders require that those who too easily have learned to be adversaries discover a new way to walk together. This book offers that new way.

FOREWORD

The Rt Rev John Pritchard, Bishop of Oxford

It's obvious that there are few parts of our national life or social experience which are not in flux at present. The only constant is change. In the 1960's (is that really fifty years ago?) Alvin Toffler was warning us in *Future Shock* that we were bumping into the future faster than we could assimilate it. What was true then is even more true today.

Unsurprisingly religious life is caught up in this ferment, not least the episcopal churches of the West, and in this book Malcolm Grundy addresses the leadership dilemmas of such churches. He puts a major challenge to those churches to recapture what he calls the 'jewel' of *episkope* before it is finally eroded by what he sees as the present vacuum in oversight and leadership, a vacuum which infects all parts of the Church's life.

I'm reminded of the observation supposedly made by Patrick Rodger, a predecessor of mine as Bishop of Oxford, who, standing in the lavatory at our Diocesan Church House, said to his neighbour, 'You know, this is about the only time in my life when I feel I really know what I'm doing, and have a pretty good chance of finishing the job.' Many bishops, in the middle of the night or in the midst of a debate in General Synod (are those the same thing?), might identify with Bishop Rodger's observation.

Malcolm Grundy argues that a rediscovery of *episcope* and a deeper understanding of what it means to belong to an episcopal family could release the church from its current mistrust and factionalism to find mutually owned solutions and new energy in following God into mission. He works carefully through different perspectives on leadership and oversight as seen from the pew, the market place and the churches, and arrives at a description of the DNA of a more fully episcopal church. I agree with so much of what he says. He puts a significant challenge to the prevailing and somewhat despairing 'but what can we do?' attitude demonstrated by so many in today's complex church life.

There seem to me to be a number of key elements in an effective, collaborative *episcope*.

1 There is no leadership in the Church without spiritual leadership. Unless the Church's leaders are passionate about the blazing reality of God, why should anyone else be interested? If God is our magnificent obsession, society will at least know what platform we speak from, and if our lives reflect that central commitment then people have the chance to be inquisitive, or even to be attracted to the revealed mystery of God. Without that, we may just be playing religious games. In Christian leadership, God matters most.

2 Oversight requires vision. The task of episcopal leadership is to gather, shape and articulate a vision which most will own because they recognize it as containing their voice. This process necessitates listening which is both broad and deep – listening both to

the people of God and to the Christian tradition, in the context of listening to our particular cultural setting. The resulting vision will then be both focused and exciting.

3 Within that clear vision, episcopal leadership needs to respect diversity and adopt a permissive style of implementation. One way of imagining how that might work is to think of the vision offering a palette of colours which parishes can use as they like to paint the particular works of art which are appropriate to the context, gifts, enthusiasms and stage of development of those churches. We don't need painting by numbers but a gallery of unique works of art.

4 A ministry of oversight requires attention to relationship even more than to organization. The latter is important; the former is essential. It comes out of a concern for the well-being of clergy and lay leaders, and a genuine desire that they should flourish. We cannot be happy when a letter in a church newspaper refers to someone retiring early on health grounds as 'lucky so-and-so'. Relationships of trust and affection can move mountains.

5 Leadership and oversight presume a shared understanding of the gift which *episcope* offers to the Church and its mission. We have to work for a situation where clergy and laity find their Christian identity within a lively episcopal ecclesiology rather than within external associations, no matter how additionally helpful they may be. In a Church where many seem determined to emphasise distinctive differences, this foundational task promises to be a long haul.

If I was to sum up these characteristics of episcopal leadership and oversight I would say that what matters most is not competence but character. What we need isn't so much good strategies as good people, and such people glow in the dark. There is no getting away from the fundamental truth that the lives of leaders are their best and worst adverts. That's why Jesus constantly probed the issue of people's inner character rather than their outward observance.

Malcolm Grundy's book is a timely stimulus to a vital area of work – the rediscovery of a theology and practice of *episcope* which bishops, clergy and laity will gladly embrace as offering coherence and missional energy to the Church. We need to build a Church where trust and accountability are given and received openly and hopefully. And it starts with the bishops themselves.

Writing in the 1830s another Bishop of Oxford, Francis Paget, wrote: 'I took this diocese solely because of its smallness, quietness and the little anxiety it need give one.' I don't recognize Oxford or any other diocese in that description today, but I'm sure that Malcolm Grundy's careful thought and acute challenges could help me make a better fist of exercising oversight in a diverse, modern diocese.

There's everything to play for.
+John Oxon

INTRODUCTION

The book which I have been able to produce has come about through the convergence of two streams of thought and experience. The first is my involvement in supporting clergy and lay people in their ministries for more than 30 years. The second is that of promoting over the same timespan ideas about how to enable change using collaborative methods of ministry with clergy, in congregations and in community projects. Both have led me to explore in some detail the problems and opportunities of being committed to a life of faith and membership in a church with a long history and well-established methods of authority and governance. These experiences of my working life merge when, with many others, I have tried to devise solutions to the questions that arise from leading churches and holding together their divided groups. Many of the old answers and solutions with their diverse justifications simply do not work any more. When they do not then they reveal gaps in our thinking.

The whole subject of the nature of oversight in episcopal churches appears to deepen rather than move towards comprehensive resolution. The debates in the Anglican Communion and elsewhere about whether or not women could be bishops, or indeed leaders at all, and about the appointment of bishops who are in stable same-sex relationships have provoked important debates about the gender of our bishops and their lifestyle. Discussion on these matters is heated and likely to continue. These controversies have obscured a more important exploration for the future of all episcopal churches. It is an exploration which needs to take place before these topical issues can ever be capable of resolution. This concerns what it is that holds together churches with episcopacy as a defining concept. More important than debating the gender and lifestyle of a bishop is the question of what bishops are for in a church whose members have come to expect participative governance and corporate leadership. This primary or fundamental exploration that I want to undertake is about how episcopal churches can explore their differences by discovering that they have an indissoluble unity through being a part of an episcopal family. That unity has to be expressed in new ways. It has to be a unity which learns how to offer the many facets and models of oversight required to lead and unify a fragmented church. Men and women, people of all races and from many cultural backgrounds have everything to offer in this reshaping of the development and oversight of our churches. How we learn to do this reshaping together will in itself be a great piece of learning about the application of leadership and oversight.

Questions can lead to the exploration of deeper and seemingly more intractable problems or they can present a range of avenues for opportunity and exploration. It seems right in introducing this book to say that I have felt the need to begin with airing some wide-ranging problems or issues in church life and only then to go on to explore the opportunities which addressing them can present. Most of the questions and issues I will explore have come to me from the many consultations and pieces of work supervision I have done. Others have come through my own experience as a church leader and as a member of local and national synods.

I will focus on one opportunity for renewal that I think is the most undervalued – that of how we can understand and use the word which gives our family of churches their name – *episkope*. The word means 'oversight' and is the first concept used by the congregations in the early church to describe the work of their leaders. From then until now it has been used for the way in which leaders in churches care for and develop their people. Its specific use in episcopal churches embraces a particular and invigorating interplay between leadership and oversight. I have become convinced that its rediscovery and consequent development could provide if not a 'catch-all' solution then at least a coherent way in which we can address our problems and explore our opportunities together.

Part of my own experience as a leader and as a consultant or mentor is that when the two streams of sensitive oversight and collaborative working methods do not come together, unfortunate patterns of behaviour result. This is understandable and able to be explained but not justified. The gaining of extra responsibility and the achievement of high office can change a person's behaviour. Many senior leaders begin to wonder who they are and ask how much the job is changing them. In a parallel way, their friends and former associates sometimes express bewilderment at a distinct change of approach and a more distanced or independent stance by a former colleague. A particularly difficult consequence for senior leaders who are unsure of their role is that internal staff relationships are affected and team thinking and joint activity become impaired. This changed behaviour may not all be 'true colours being revealed at last' but the result of a combination of an unreflective copying of a leadership model from another walk of life combined with the lack of a full enough understanding of the nature and procedures of the kind of leadership and oversight which is expected.

It is not without some trepidation that have I tiptoed into the province of church governance. In a search for literature to describe how churches with a hierarchy of bishops and archbishops are constructed, I became surprised by how little has been written in recent times. There are, of course, very many biographies and autobiographies about the lives of bishops. These describe their upbringing, their training and their networks of friends and colleagues. All talk about the work which bishops have done and many quote extensively from their writings. It has been interesting, and for my study illuminating, to see that there is very little reflection by the authors of these books or by the bishops themselves about what it actually means to become a bishop – or a church leader as archdeacon or cathedral dean – in an episcopal church.

In a similar way I looked for theological and ecclesiological contributions to our understanding of how episcopal churches work and the particular role of bishops and other senior leaders. There were many pieces on the practicalities of what church leaders are expected to do. There are controversies throughout history about the place of bishops in the wider societies of many countries and some of them are well documented. These were more about their interventions in the politics of their day or their work for justice and on behalf of the underprivileged than about the nature of the office and work itself. The thinking about church structures and senior responsibilities can be found as guidance notes in letters between bishops and archbishops in the early church, and latterly in discussions between denominations as they considered relationships with one another. Theology and 'job descriptions' are contained in the words used in the ordinals when priests are ordained and when bishops are consecrated. These give a liturgical and a theological foundation but leave all to be worked out in practice.

The discovery of this absence of writing about the role and work of a senior church leader led me to look at many of the recently published reviews of appointment systems and support mechanisms for those who are called to these offices of responsibility. As might be expected, there is much history in them and significant quarrying of the writings about bishops and theologians from the early church to the present day. While appointment systems have been put under the microscope, no-one has gone behind these to explore what the work of a senior church leader needs to look like in the modern world.

The serious 'corporate' consequence following from a lack of understanding about what is needed from those who are our leaders is that a whole raft of different ideas, expectations and projections come to the surface. The result is that there is far more disagreement than focus about what bishops and other senior staff are for, and how best they support and enable the mission and ministry of the churches. When there is no mutually understood view about the nature of a leadership, then fragmentation begins to appear and power groups from inside and outside the structures of a church can become inappropriately dominant.

In the chapters of this book I have set out my thinking by first describing some of the vacuums in leadership and oversight in our churches as I have experienced them in the various aspects of my work. I go on to ask why *episkope* could be a particularly important part of any solution. After that I look at the origins of episcopal ministry and at the history and theology which explain its development. Following on from those initial pieces of deep digging I have tried to describe how episcopally structured churches can be viewed 'from the pew' and then to see how ministries of oversight can be exercised 'in the market place'. Most exhilarating has been the discovery that a renewed understanding of *episkope* can be evidenced and justified through a surprisingly coherent series of ecumenical agreements over the past 50 years. Essential has been an examination of the temptations which come with power, and a brief look at the spiritualities which can combat them. I conclude with my own perhaps all too strident view of what steps episcopal churches need to take for the future.

My trepidation in undertaking this writing is about venturing into territory which so few have reflected on before. I may well be guilty of the accusation that 'fools rush in where angels fear to tread' and on occasions of making unverified assumptions. Nevertheless, even if much of what I say is more challenging than informative, I hope that I will have begun to open up territory which those who are more capable can explore. I have chosen to look in great detail at a word and a concept that seems to me to offer a way forward and that, in churches with the title or within the family called 'episcopal', might seem all too obvious.

Without these much needed pieces of work there will remain only partial and even merely anecdotal sources of information and guidance for newly appointed leaders. There are very few places where people appointed to senior posts can go for support in their work and where they can reflect on it. There are similar absences for those who have been in post for a number of years. In an associated way there is far too much reserve about identifying and developing those who might become leaders for the next generation in our churches. As a consequence the learning curve for those appointed can be challengingly steep. Conflicts arise and appear to be perpetuated in some cases because the skills needed for overseeing such a diverse organization have not been discovered or learned. Other issues remain unresolved simply because a common bond and commitment to the oversight of a denomination is lacking. In churches with episcopal structures there is a particular way in which these absences can be addressed, and I have tried to look throughout this book at what could be done to make solutions clearer.

As in all other modern organizations leadership cannot be held by one person and in one place. It has to be shared between groups and staff teams who are each given their own areas of responsibility, with the person at the top guiding and representing the work of the whole. Episcopal churches have a historic and particular understanding of how the centralized and the distributed parts of a church can work together. When this understanding works well, with trust and energy flowing from one part to the other, they can be amazingly effective. I want to explore in this book what such a revitalized concept of *episkope* would look like if it were re-evaluated and re-presented as a way of giving acceptable meaning and purpose for the work of our churches.

I

The Vacuum in Leadership and Oversight

Something has gone wrong in the life of our churches. Among the international community of episcopal churches there has developed a culture of internal mistrust which exists even when differences have not come to the surface. There is a gulf between the life and concerns of local congregations and the ways in which those with wider leadership responsibility organize and run them. For many people in many different places, this manifests itself in episcopal churches in what I describe as a series of vacuums in leadership. The result of these absences is the lack of any feeling of joint responsibility for the leadership and governance of our churches. These culminate in an absence of shared oversight – the very thing which should be of the essence of any church which has *episkope* as its fundamental uniting concept.

Episcopal churches belong to an international family. Their similarities might suggest that they have a common and binding relationship with one another. Their clear and describable characteristics, tested through the centuries with bishops as the chief overseers,

mark them out as being different from other church groupings. They
have common types of church order and lines of accountability. They
call, ordain and consecrate their leaders by ancient tradition and after
a certain amount of consultation. There is every reason to think that
these episcopal churches know how to lead in an international way,
that they have time-honoured ways of settling their differences and
that they know what it is that binds them together. That is not the
case at all. This commonality of relationship has become honoured
more in name than in practice. Relationships between members of
the episcopal family of churches are at best fragile. The machinery
of episcopal governance and oversight does not seem to be able to
hold together member churches in an effective way any more. The
underlying concept of unity is broken and the different parts are
attempting to work on their own. There are many places where this
brokenness in the workings of the machinery can be detected. There
is not one fault; there are many, and in many different places.

An essential part of the way in which episcopal churches are
organized is that they have taken the concept of *episkope* and made
it central to the way in which they understand themselves. *Episkope*
comes from the amalgamation of two Greek words, meaning 'over'
and 'seeing'. It is the defining concept of a denomination which does
not want its congregations to regard themselves as independent units
but which has as its fundamental philosophy that there is a living
relationship between each and all. This relationship extends itself to
mean that there is a mutuality of responsibility between each congregation, deanery and diocese and that each acknowledges a sharing in
oversight of the other. One of the most alarming characteristics of
episcopal churches in our generation is that they appear to have lost
the memory about what it is that binds them together. This loss can
be described as a vacuum in the understanding of what it means to be
an episcopalian. The use of this word is more common in the United
States than anywhere else. In other places members of episcopal
churches might call themselves Anglican or Lutheran – or, of course,
Roman Catholic or Orthodox. The loss of memory of this defining

concept is serious. I am going to explore whether or not the remembering or the rediscovery of *episkope* can become one of the principal ways in which the vacuum in appropriate leadership and oversight can be relieved.

The vacuum in leadership

There is a vacuum in our understanding of how episcopal churches are led. One of the most serious events of recent times in church life, and a significant part of the reason for engaging in this study, is the gap which has been created in the practice of being an appointed leader, and the community which gives meaning, value and legitimacy to that role. This is not to say that individual bishops and their staff do not cope well with the jobs they are given. It is that the structures of a diocese and of national churches, as well as the roles which church members force on senior leaders, prevent them from exercising the kind of leadership and oversight the churches need – and which many of those appointed would want to give.

At a local level, and I have checked this out with many clergy and lay people, the view has been expressed that until recently, bishops and archdeacons and certainly cathedral deans were thought of as benevolent if rather distant figures. Lay people on the whole liked or wanted to like their bishops even if they only met them on a few public occasions such as confirmations and inductions. They tell me that all this has changed. There is now a much more generalized suspicion of bishops and other senior leaders as those who represent changes to church life which are not negotiated well. Discussions abut reducing the provision of clergy and the scarcity of resources are seen to diminish effectiveness and are imposed upon local congregations at a time when faith commitment is stronger than ever and they contribute considerably more in financial terms. The problem is a structural and not a personal one reflecting any kind of inadequacy, though better training would always be welcomed. Behind these impressions there is a theological concern about the ways in which the Church can and perhaps should understand *episkope*. All those with any concern about how episcopal churches are led and governed are looking for a place to begin again, rebuild trust and negotiate change.

Essential to any description of a church, just like any other modern organization, is an understanding of who its leaders are and of how it is led. One symptom of brokenness in the episcopal family of churches is that, although there are leaders with impressive and ancient titles, no-one quite knows who the real leaders are and where influential initiatives are coming from. In episcopal churches the named leaders – archbishops, bishops, archdeacons and cathedral deans – still have a high public profile and much acclamation from devout and faithful followers – but only if they fit the models their followers have created for them and do not stray too far from the 'party line' towards radicalism, innovation or even eccentricity! The result of such constraint or restriction is that leadership in the churches has lost a sense of direction, spends much time in resolving disputes and has little spare energy for vision and development. It is not too much of an exaggeration to say that people in the episcopal family of churches live in a leadership vacuum. That is not to say there is no leadership, though that may be the case in some parishes, deaneries and dioceses; it is more that there are many kinds of leader in many different places and parts of the church and that they are pulling or leading in many different directions. There is not enough time for strategic thinking and for making a difference in the wider world. Such an exhaustion of energy frustrates and neutralizes leadership.

Knowing how to lead in the place of responsibility given is an art and a science. Its practice has an inner and an outer face. One exudes confidence and shows a public face which is clear and determined, able to make tough decisions and take followers into new places of achievement. The other face, usually more known to the leader than to the led, is unsure and feeling the way forward a step at a time, not always knowing which solutions will work and whether support or sabotage and betrayal will come from friends or from foes. The leadership dilemma is a familiar one and both of its faces will be part of the privilege and responsibility of leadership for many wherever extra responsibility has been won or thrust upon the hopeful or the unsuspecting.

There is another element in the way a Christian leader sees and feels their responsibility; is God's spirit and their church calling them out from a place where they are confident and even comfortable to do something which may not be of their own choosing? They may only know this if they have the confidence to see and respond to what God may or may not be leading them to do. Wisdom based on experience is one of the most significant requirements in any leader. With all this confidence, where then does the present confusion and vacuum in church leadership originate?

The vacuum in oversight

The oversight of any denomination is important, and different Christian traditions have taken their own decisions about how they are structured. Oversight is not just a term in episcopal churches for mutual recognition or responsibility. It describes a particular way in which these churches are structured and governed. The vacuum described here is one where a sense of organized authority willingly accepted as oversight is no longer there. In an age of democratic institutions and of wide participation in decision making, there is a definite need to re-examine how this kind of authority structure can work. It is just possible that the list of aspects of brokenness which I am describing means that another way of organizing and governing churches may have to be found, or will emerge. This would be one which is more in keeping with contemporary expectations about how voluntary and public institutions work. It would be a radical departure.

Alternatively, it could be that a renewed and rediscovered use of the concept of an *episkope* which embraces a mutuality of

understanding and respect between groups of people could be a
new model for emerging church governance. It would fill a vacuum.
Leadership is always embodied in human form and is always open to
distortion and corruption. An outmoded practice from history and a
vacuum in contemporary understanding do not necessarily lead to
the conclusion that the concept is unworkable. Identifying a vacuum
in the understanding and application of *episkope* can open up for all
churches a debate about the best way for each to be governed. If
episcopal churches are to contribute to that debate with any depth
of understanding then we all need an exploration of this kind to
learn again what it is about our valuing of oversight – and episcopal
oversight – which we would want to keep.

There could be another view and it might say that the wide range of
leadership initiatives and interpretations of church which we have at the
present time are part of a redefining and remaking of Christendom or
at least of the Church. The many experiments and break-away groups
each taking a view on a non-negotiable matter of principle, usually about
a single issue, are creating a new kind of ecclesiastical culture. We
could call it the 'fragmented whole', the unfreezing of outdated
structures or the creation of a new kind of ecclesial episcopal church.
This may well be the case. In one sense it is an accurate account of
what is happening. However, if this is a permanent pattern which
defines a fragmented Church with an individually interpreted and
dispersed leadership, there are serious questions about how such a
reality relates to the inclusive acceptance of *episkope* which assumes
an underlying unity of belief and a transparent and widely accepted
form of governance.

No group of Christians who have a fundamental belief in
episcopacy as the basis for unity could assent to such a re-forming
situation with any happiness or ease. While all would agree that the
life of parishes and congregations is the bedrock of the church, there
have to be additional characteristics which hold episcopal churches
together. Central to all of these is *episkope* – how a uniformity of
oversight is exercised; to what extent it is shared by the whole

Body; and where particular functions are focused for those who are appointed and trusted with leadership.

The vacuum in relationship

All organizations rely on interaction of some kind. Even 'virtual' ones require participation and response. Churches are the places where activity and beliefs are built on relationship. People in their many types and with their various hopes and expectations are the life-blood of the church. It has to be that those who are called to any kind of responsibility in any church depend more than anything else on the quality of relationship they have with those for whom they are responsible, for whom they have oversight. Church leaders have to relate to their clergy and people in particular ways. They are the focus of hope and expectation; they are the encouragers and the affirmers; they decide who will be admitted to office and they exercise discipline. It is possible to attempt each of these things at a distance and largely through other people in impersonal ways – but not for long and not in completely effective ways. There is a difference between trusted delegation and abrogation – the avoidance of hands-on activity. The busyness of senior leaders and the pressures placed upon them by their churches make it less and less easy for them to establish confident working relationships with their people. Yet the hope that a leader can be felt to be known and that they are accessible when needed is a core element of a church built on trusted relationships.

There is evidence that these relationships of trust are not fully in place and that local congregations and communities are beginning to notice this. If a bishop or an archdeacon is only met to negotiate a change in local church life which results in a reduction in resources and clergy, then something essential is missing, especially if the reduction is inadequately negotiated. One of the publications which I edited and published when director of the Foundation for Church Leadership was an impassioned essay on the absence of good relationships within the church by David Brown. He had been a senior naval officer and then personal assistant to two Bishops of Lichfield. His sensitively articulated opinion, well researched and argued, was that bishops were prevented from being what they are intended to be for the churches, and especially in his case for the Church of England, because ecclesiastical structures and the burden of expectations in 'running' a diocese forced them into an uncomfortable mould. His conclusion was that bishops were trapped into inappropriate roles and functions, hence the title of his booklet published by FCL: *Releasing Bishops for Relationship*.[1]

In telling phrases he says,

> … who is there to release bishops from the hindrances that have accumulated at their door, often preventing their getting out and alongside – and even knowing – those they serve? Maybe the institution has gained a fraudulent trust so that its hindrances are revered rather than removed; scarcely noted or weighed.
>
> The penalty of such hindrances may be seen in the erosion of episcopal standing and thence influence, in work patterns that hazard spiritual, personal and family well-being …
>
> Now, as ever, the Church's treasure matches precisely the surrounding human need; but unless God's people and Church leaders accept the priority of relationship, this chasm cannot be bridged. As things stand, the Church too often proclaims love but portrays fragmentation and disagreement from the international to the local level.
>
> When a military formation is found to be in the wrong place for its developing task, it needs repositioning – fast! That is the challenge of leadership.

The repositioning, he says, requires that the 'second order' priorities which distance bishops from their people need to be exposed since they masquerade as 'first order' priorities. His view is that the 'first order' priorities for the person appointed as bishop are all about the building and rebuilding of relationships within the church and between the church and its surrounding community. First order priorities are about establishing relationships which make *episkope* a living experience. Other staff who are sharing in *episkope* need to be seen to be undertaking tasks with and for their bishop.

This theme has been taken up by Dr Lorraine Cavanagh in a book also with an impassioned theme. It is one which also tries to address the vacuum in relationship. She believes that the fragile relationships between bishops and members of the Anglican Communion need to be restored by rediscovering bonds of affection. In a study of the nature of Anglicanism leading to the events of the Lambeth Conference of Anglican bishops in 2008: *By One Spirit: Reconciliation and Renewal in Anglican life*, she is moving towards an understanding of the problem.[2] She can see that part of the cause of the vacuum in relationships is a forgetting of what the bonds are which hold the Anglican Communion together. She asks for a rediscovery of the spirituality which understands again what it is that binds people in these churches together. In a time of reflection and with a moratorium on further divisive meetings, she hopes that through the deliberate use of listening techniques some semblance of charity might be restored. Her ultimate aim is that Anglicans relearn the ways in which they can share and experience hospitality. While perceptive and vital, this alone will not fill the vacuum in a way which will bring about lasting change. It will create the right conditions. The change needed is the rediscovery of what it is that binds episcopal churches together. Spirituality and hospitality alone will not restore a belief in *episkope* as the unifying element in this denomination. What is needed is a repositioning of understandings of relatedness that will lead to a willingness to share responsibility for leadership and oversight across this Communion.

The vacuum in diocesan leadership

Current interpretations of what it means specifically to be a bishop and how to exercise that ministry are closely linked to history, traditional expectations and to personal interpretation. These do not always produce a happy result. Just as many clergy and members of congregations no longer seem to have the love and respect for their bishops which once existed, so also many bishops do not find it clear or easy to establish a right relationship with their parishes. It is becoming extremely difficult to lead a diocese when significant numbers of its membership disagree in a fundamental way with their bishop's theology and understanding of church. In many dioceses this has produced a debilitating paradox; in the place where leadership might be expected to be exercised, the senior staff team, we have something completely different. The senior team is selected to reflect 'difference' in a diocese rather than the pastoral, mission and strategic needs of the moment. Within many senior teams there is a lack of strategic coherence. There can be found someone who is firmly against the ordination of women, a woman priest who is a dean or archdeacon, a suffragan bishop who is an evangelical and a diocesan who is from the catholic tradition, or vice versa. Some of these teams do work effectively and everything hangs on the chemistry of those appointed and their ability to get on with one another. Other senior teams are significantly dysfunctional, with party games being played out and predetermined positions being defended. Constituencies expect the person in the senior team to represent their interests rather than to become welded into a strategic group which will take the diocese or the province on to a new place.

There is a vacuum here, and the way to fill it is not with individual initiatives from entrepreneurial bishops or with a catalogue of further complaints about the way things are in our episcopally led churches, nor even with a book about self-help. The way forward is for a re-imagining of the concept of *episkope* and with it an examination of what leadership and oversight might look like in a church which can develop its heritage and its traditions in order to understand itself in a different way. *Episkope* is definitely something that requires a two-way relationship. In this respect it is not unlike any other form of leadership. There has to be a reciprocal relationship between the person who is appointed leader and the people under their care. Leaders gain respect and authority through the way they carry out their responsibilities. They build credibility through the person they are and the decisions they take. This personality is structured by core beliefs and values. If these are seen to inform decisions and actions, then a leader might well be described as a person acting with integrity, however hard the decisions are that they have to make.

When pragmatism, party loyalty and undue compromise characterize decisions, then credibility and respect diminish, and sometimes integrity is brought into question; a vacuum of confidence begins to be created. What appears to be lacking in the public structure of episcopal churches is a mechanism to assess the performance of a senior leader. Review programmes do exist and archbishops do carry our ministerial reviews of the bishops in their care. But there remains an absence of procedures that will address the 'square peg' situation in a rigorous and appropriately public way.

The vacuum in vocational understanding

There is no longer a consensus view about what a bishop should be or what they should do. Quite distressingly, we are now in an international situation among many episcopally led dioceses and provinces where the bishop has become a focus of division and party interest rather than of unity. It is no wonder that we are at a time when the work of bishops needs to be reviewed. Questions have been asked in a pragmatic way about their number and cost, but there are more fundamental questions. As divisions deepen over a range of issues – homosexuality, the place of women, interpretations of the Bible, the public lifestyle of ministers and much more – we have to ask whether the personal figure of a bishop can bear the weight of expectations placed upon them, and if they can continue to be the primary – and sometimes the exclusive – focus of authority and for unity in our churches.

The vacuum is a serious one and is the energizing motive for this book. It has been part of the sad and challenging experiences of my life to see good and well-meaning people appointed as bishops only to see them changed almost beyond recognition within months rather than years of their taking up office. Many reasons exist for this; one of these is that there is a very strong culture of 'bishoping' which exaggerates and emphasizes difference between holders of this office and any other. I observe how little is in place as support structures for new bishops, and how few of them engage in whatever in-service training is available. There are not many opportunities for bishops and other senior leaders to meet in order to reflect on their role and their position in the church which has called them. When these opportunities are not available then these leaders look for support to like-minded colleagues and to those who affirm their ministries out of party allegiance. All of this separates them from a wide range of colleagues and congregations and causes a vacuum in integrated leadership.

As groups splinter away from dioceses and as non-geographical dioceses could just possibly become established, we have to ask if it is appropriate for any episcopally ordained person to foster or relate to such divisions, let alone become the representative of a faction or splinter group. Can we have a church of the future where priests, lay people and whole congregations can choose their own bishop rather than work at being part of a more comprehensive and locally-based whole?

The vacuum in episcopal leadership centres on the ways in which our bishops have understood their calling and their responsibility in this present age. We must look at the kind of church and society that make them what they are. It is essential that we put under a magnifying glass the changes that we can see taking place, and through that analysis begin to describe a changing church as we see it. There has to be criticism and contradiction in the pictures that will be painted. Part of the chaos which appears to be a characteristic of change is shown in different forms of episcopal leadership in our churches. Some will endure and make a part of the new shape for a future church. Others will be seen as for their day or time only and be a perhaps necessary distraction or accommodation in order that the main tasks of *episkope* in leadership can be accomplished.

As we set out on our exploration we can only acknowledge that there is a great frustration with the work and achievements of bishops and those staff with whom they share *episkope* as we see and experience them. Perhaps some of this frustration comes about through our own lack of knowledge about what we can expect from them, as from any of our leaders. On many occasions we have forced them into difficult and uncomfortable places. Without more support, many are not equipped to work out who they are and how they should respond in pressurized and changing times. Some are content to hide in the comfort of their own security, be it of party allegiance or in the trappings of role and function, and this too is unacceptable.

We are all in part to blame, but we are not all called to be reformers. Some are just called to put down a marker that there is a problem and that if it is not addressed our churches – and their ministry and mission – will suffer. What we do all need to know is more about the structure and nature of episcopal churches. They have not always been as they are now and they do not need to continue with their present ways and practices. In order to know where we have come from in appointing our episcopal leaders, and how we should develop and select those who will be the next generation of leaders, we need to acknowledge that we have a problem: that there is a vacuum in our understanding and reception of episcopal leadership. Unless we are sure about how oversight will need to be exercised in our churches for the future, further distortions will sweep in to fill the vacuum and the there will be a consequent lack of clarity about how to identify and select our leaders.

The congregational vacuum

There is a vacuum or a yawning chasm between many congregations with their ministers and diocesan or centralized leadership. Congregations do not feel resourced, enabled and inspired by those in senior responsible positions in dioceses. Instead they perceive central intervention as interference and financial requests as a tax rather than as a contribution to the overall mission and ministry of a diocese.

What is it that newcomers to congregational life are invited to 'belong' to? One of the most significant places where there is a vacuum lies between the local congregations housed in buildings called churches and new, more informal, groups of people; they would in many cases not recognize themselves as congregations. These are often in what are called 'Fresh Expressions' of church led by a new type of appointment, a Pioneer Minister. The two manifestations of mission and ministry have yet to cohere as part of one church. A number of leaders in the new church movements have now come into mainstream senior church leadership. The vacuum here is in the absence of creative dialogue between leaders formed in the 'inherited church' and those shaped by and more committed to the 'emerging church'. Most ministers have to manage and lead both, and this places them in situations of considerable tension. Episcopal leadership, expressing oversight over both, is presented with significant bridge building challenges here.[3]

There is a completely appropriate tension between the local and the universal church. Vibrant local congregations led by able clergy and responsible lay people are the only way in which the church can live any real life. Their loyalty is to the congregation as a beacon of hope and faith to those around. However understandable, excessive local allegiance, often with a sense of envy and rivalry with the neighbouring congregations and a low commitment to deanery activities, lessens or eradicates much of a sense of belonging to something which has a wider frame of reference and which actually gives the defining shape and structure to the local church.

In many countries of Western Europe there is a shortage of stipendiary (paid) clergy. This has a number of consequences. It does not necessarily mean that there are fewer clergy in a diocese. It means that a significant number are non-stipendiary or self-supporting. They are not necessarily as deployable, but are enormously committed. These priests are colleagues with a large number of lay people licensed to take services, and a whole range of ordained and non-ordained specialist workers. Such a significant spectrum of church personnel means that the life of the local church has changed already. One significant vacuum is the lack of recognition about this change in the structures of the dioceses. Most – almost all – of those in senior leadership have taken the full-time, stipendiary route and do not necessarily find it easy to adjust to this new situation. Meetings, deployment strategies, synods and consultation processes are still very biased towards the stipendiary clergy. There is a vacuum of recognition here.

The vacuum in shared oversight

Equally significant is the way in which future planning is carried out and where *episkope* is expected to be exercised. There has been a significant shift towards using deaneries as the place for debate, but not always where decisions are made about deployment of clergy and the grouping of parishes. In such a situation there is an inevitable tendency for anxiety, mistrust and rivalry to emerge. Here, quite as much as anywhere else, there is a need for the discovery of the deeper meanings of *episkope*. Without a deeply held sense of mutual responsibility and a genuine desire to re-shape the local church for effective mission and ministry, fragmentation – or a vacuum in the willingness to think together about the future – has to be the inevitable consequence. Leadership and oversight have to be both local and regional, with recognized lines of communication and trusted ways of decision making. There will always be a tension between those with the local view and those with a wider perspective. It can lead to healthy debate and creative solutions or it can lead to mistrust and frustration among all concerned.

This vacuum in the understanding of shared oversight shows itself in many ways and not least when the minister leaves and

consultations have to take place. Is the deanery plan taken seriously
or is it 'capped' by external interests which confirm the suspicion
that the deanery is not really trusted to carry out and execute its own
planning? As with other parts of the world, there are negotiations
with the diocese, and then in England sometimes with a 'Patron',
sometimes a local family, an Oxford or Cambridge college, a trust
representing a church party or the Crown and the representatives of
the monarch, all of whom still 'own' the living and have a right to
suggest the next vicar. Many members of congregations involved in
the appointment of their new minister will be unfamiliar with this
process. They will not all have an Anglican background and can only
have a distant acquaintance with some of those who now descend
on them and become involved in the appointment. The glue that
should and must hold this together is the other side of the concept
of *episkope*: that there are responsible and appointed or chosen people
who have a wider responsibility for the maintenance of the faith in an
area than that of the congregation which will, understandably, have
a primary focus on its own needs. Similar issues emerge with the
selection and choice of a new bishop. These questions about another
element of *episkope* will be addressed in a later chapter.

There is an equal and often just as heated series of questions
posed when money has to be taken from the congregation to pay for
the activities and work of a diocese and of the wider national church.
Resentment about the levy – called quota or more aptly the 'share' –
is rife, and affects other views of belonging to something wider than
the local with its particular needs for ministry. There are many layers
to the acceptance of *episkope* and some of these can be reflected in a
two-way reciprocity. 'Bear ye one another's burdens' (Gal. 6.2.) can
be a deep-seated concept that enables oversight to move forward to
a willing acceptance of mutual support and of subsidy, or seed corn
investment in weak or missionary parishes. Churches in Northern
Europe, once fully supported by a Church Tax, are discovering the
need for this in sometimes painful ways.

Local clergy have a particular role in accepting, supporting and developing the concepts of leadership and oversight. Many will have come into ministry as a second career and will be used to accountability and to working as part of a wider structure. Many will have managed bringing up a family and holding together a home before ordination alongside life in their church. Almost all will have come to ordination through a strong call to a 'pastoral' ministry of some kind and very often through a role model of their local priest or minister or from an amalgam of several ministers over a number of years. This non-church reference point and wider set of responsibilities will have given the strong sense that direction is given to a company from much wider than one department and that family life is challenging and complex. All these experiences come into an ecclesiastical understanding of leadership and oversight and have the potential to renew it.

There has to be a wider frame of reference which oversees and develops any church. A vacuum is created where the willingness to accept a wider frame of reference is resented and where the local congregation wants to go its own way. The authority to lead and give oversight in the community as well as in the congregation comes in episcopal churches from underlying concepts of a 'ministry to all in the community' through the wider obligation to lead and to oversee which is embodied in the structure of a parish, a diocese and its synod, and in the role and representative function of its bishops. It is this wider concept of shared oversight which has been eroded and caused a distressing vacuum.

The synodical vacuum

We have a vacuum of belief that synodical systems can resolve the major issues of leadership or oversight facing the churches. In history synods have played a key role in settling differences. Todays synodical government has become a kind of 'parliament' with opposing 'parties' debating their different positions on controversial issues. This is resourced by a beaurocratic kind of structure which gives order but over-formalizes business and decision making. There is even a view that many of the internal church issues which take up much time in synodical meetings divert the churches from addressing issues of greater concern to the wider world. That alone would indicate a loss of the sense of responsibility or oversight in God's world. As a consequence, these structures, with their loss of the sense of shared oversight, stifle any prophetic voice.

The concept of Democratic Network Governance has recently come to my attention. It may well provide a solution in modern, complex church organizations to perplexing and frustrating issues about the implementation of change. The essence of episcopally led and synodically governed churches is the link between oversight and governance. The broad arguments for this concept are set out in an accessible way by an international symposium of Political and Social Scientists from Europe and the USA in a collection of essays called *Theories of Democratic Network Governance*.[4]

In a relatively new field of research, Democratic Network Governance has its origins in research into how progress is made and strategies developed and implemented in non-hierarchical types of organization where many different groups have a considerable say, both positively and negatively, in implementing change. The origins of this research are in a study of the interaction between public, semi-public and private sector organizations in public decision-making processes. Similarities between the negotiation, implementation or otherwise in diocesan and national church structures are striking. These similarities, with examples, will be explored towards the end of chapter VI.

The discovery that governing processes are not fully controlled by those 'in charge' of the governing or leadership levers in an organization can hardly come as a complete surprise. Why leaders and leadership teams cannot be in charge and command direction in large, complex modern organizations that are also subject to lobbying and public pressure is the subject of research in Democratic

Network Governance. The significant conclusion of such studies is that the implementation of change or the delivery of a strategy is subject to complex negotiations between public and private sector groups who belong to organizations that are relatively stable.

The vital link between those who are involved in implementing change and those subject to the changes is that while being operationally autonomous, independent and self-governing, *each is dependent on the resources and capacities to deliver of the other.* In much the same way, bishops and their staff teams and the Bishop's Councils within Synodical Government are dependent on the capacity to deliver of parish congregations, and their ability and willingness to fund the activities of a diocese. Diocesan structures are in their turn dependent on the goodwill, funding grant aid and permissions from conservation and heritage organizations for their buildings, on national, regional and local government for the funding of many community projects and major voluntary sector partners for the delivery of welfare and community facilities. No one group is able to act alone; each is in one way or another dependent on the other and each can block or frustrate progress.

Member groups of interacting organizations do not work with or against one another in a vacuum. They work within a national or regional network of authoritative bodies that when interacting effectively produce results that are more than the sum of their parts. The cement which binds them together is a commitment to the 'production of public purpose' within an area. Public Purpose is the expression of visions, values, plans and policies within the confines of a particular network. The development and delivery of policy and strategy is achieved through political negotiations with those involved to identify emerging policy issues or to address and solve particular community problems. Networks which do not contribute, by choice or through deliberate action, cannot be regarded as participants in governance networks.

Episcopally structured national churches have no choice but to be a part of national and regional governance networks, and their chosen leaders do need to gain some experience in this area. Equally, the lessons learned from such participation illustrate and inform how leadership has to be negotiated in dioceses and in national and international churches. Oversight cannot be understood by leaders and change cannot be brought about without this understanding of democratic network governance.

The acid test of the effective working of a governance network is the compliance with and commitment to collectively negotiated decisions. Sensitively carried through by leaders who can command respect, politically negotiated agreements can gain assent within church circles where member groups hold differing theological views. Similarly negotiated decisions can mobilize groups made up of paid employees and volunteers such as those in large parish churches or cathedrals. A later chapter will look at *episkope* and leadership by bishops and others in what they call 'the market place'. They can learn much about mutually beneficial working relationships from theories of Democratic Network Governance. A vacuum can be filled in the most appropriate and effective way, and leaders from parish priest to bishop can discover the key which will open doors to greater effectiveness.

The identity vacuum

Cataloguing a list of deficiencies and inadequacies all adds up to a vacuum in the ways in which we understand, lead and develop our episcopal churches. There is also a significant and more fundamentally serious vacuum in the understanding of how churches relate to their wider communities in ways which build relationships and create mutually beneficial partnerships. To use a technical word, there is a vacuum in the understanding of ecclesiology. To fill this vacuum in the most beneficial way it is necessary to explore existing models of church and describe some others that are emerging, and which might become the building blocks of self-understanding for individuals and for congregations as new patterns of local and national leadership are formed. A redefined ecclesiology will lead to an appropriate filling of the vacuum in understanding of leadership and oversight. It will contribute to a redressing of the balance in the creation of churches which have *episkope* as a means of governance which is representative of the membership and which speaks with clarity and confidence in a world where the Christian faith can still be influential.

The challenge for anyone who is either a leader or a follower in their church is to determine what the main purpose of the organization is, and to what extent its stated aims can be witnessed from its activities. One unified leadership going in the same direction would be a foolish proposition and impossible to achieve. In this study of episcopally led churches, the essence of a common structure and view of what leadership and oversight represent is that shared core beliefs and values give permission for trusted development along differing avenues. Without this – and there is evidence that it does not exist in sufficient quantity in our episcopally led churches today – a vacuum becomes filled with bids for leadership from many different places. Power groups, representing one or even a minority view, gain publicity and attract dissident followers. They distort and divide while presuming to offer a way forward which might unite, but only around a partial view of what a universal, all-embracing, church needs to be. Without recognizable and accepted forms of leadership episcopal churches will struggle to defend their difference and their comprehensiveness.

In order to look at the places where behaviour has become inappropriate and where the mechanism to settle disputes and plan for the future has become disconnected, it has been important to look first at the many places where leadership and oversight are not working in the governance of our episcopal churches. A wrong approach would be to attribute blame or to rush into another set of practical solutions. The right thing to do has been to describe how the problems manifest themselves by describing the vacuums which are created and some of the symptoms displayed. In naming some or many specific areas in this way, I want to create opportunities for analysis and diagnosis. Descriptions of the activities of the necessary parts of our church need to be unfolded in order that some cohesiveness can be brought to how we support and care for one another. But first we do need to discover what bishops are, where they have come from and what *episkope* has meant at other times and in other places. We must examine the models of episcopal leadership which have served the church for better or for worse through the centuries and made it what it is today.

Notes

1 Brown, David, *Releasing Bishops for Relationship*, Foundation for Church Leadership, 2008 pp. 7 & 8.
2 Cavanagh, Lorraine, *By One Spirit: Reconciliation and Renewal in Anglican Life*. Peter Lang, 2009.
3 See a great volume of literature begun by significant books such as Warren, Robert, *Building Missionary Congregations*; Finney, John, *Finding Faith Today*, *Mission-shaped Church: Church Planting and Fresh Expressions of Church in a Changing Context*, Church House Publishing, and a critique by Hull, John, *Mission-shaped Church: a Theological Response*. SCM, 2006.
4 See Sørensen, Eva and Torfing, Jacob (ed.), *Theories of Democratic Network Governance*, Palgrave MacMillan, 2008.

II

Episkope – a new old idea

I have come to the conclusion that because there has not been enough thinking about the workings of episcopal churches, many leaders have not been enabled to understand the history and culture of the church in which they have become a senior figure. As a consequence of this lack of thinking, many clergy and church members are less than clear about why they should show allegiance to a church with episcopacy as its core characteristic. I can now see that what we need is a theological idea that will energize and inform ways of being a family of episcopal churches for the future. It will resolve the many vacuums which frustrate so many.

There is a way in which we can transform the many frustrations which prevent progress in the effective working of our churches. It begins with an acknowledgement that being a leader in today's church is complex and problematic. In his first sermon as Bishop of St Albans in 1970, Robert Runcie took full advantage of a misprint about his enthronement in the local newspaper:

I confess that there have been times in the past few weeks when I have wondered whether I was being made a baron or a bishop, and there have been times when I wondered whether an inspired misprint in a local paper which referred to my 'enthornment' did not do more justice to the prickly seat on which a bishop must sit these days.

But that was not all. He went on to describe just what a different kind of episcopal leadership in a different kind of church needs to be like. Forty years later the challenge remains:

It would be easy to deplore the collapse of authorities. It may be more helpful to explore a new style of leadership geared at helping people to do things for themselves, to lead their community and transform and renew it not from the outside but from within … It would be more helpful to recognize that the church is a servant and not a rival to society. It is the capacity to inspire which matters.[1]

Leadership in episcopal churches

Episcopally led churches have someone, in many parts of the world now a man or a woman, called a bishop or an archbishop at the top of their structure. They are chosen to be a figurehead and a representative person to lead, care for and guide the personnel and membership of what have become large organizations where power and responsibility is distributed in many different places. The most senior people in episcopal churches are bishops and archbishops. They are the public face of a religion which is motivated by beliefs and values and which promotes a vision of the greater good. On occasion it tries to regulate personal and corporate behaviour in society, emphasizing rules for community living which protect the vulnerable and inspire the renegotiation of corporately held values. In common with all churches of every kind it invites people to a faith in God as known in the pages of the Bible and through the life and teachings of Jesus Christ – a continuing experience to this present day.

Episcopal churches, in addition to having bishops and archbishops as their senior figures, have synods, made up of representatives of the laity and of the clergy where, at local and national level, major issues concerning the life of the church are debated. The balance between the leadership given by bishops and the debates and decisions made by synods often creates a tension. In arguments which will be described later in this book, some ecclesiastical ways of leading and governing jar very painfully with the expectations of modern participative organizations, and on occasion challenge legislation designed to safeguard and protect employment and the rights of vulnerable groups. As a result of this it has become imperative that an extended study of how and why episcopal churches work as they do is carried out.

Learning about *episkope*

Newly appointed church leaders, not always with a background in the complexities of church or cathedral life, have a steep learning curve. The technicalities of the role have to be learned, while at the same time the new occupant is thrust into public life and expected to pronounce on any number of issues. Many church leaders say that there are hardly any places where they can discuss and explore their role with appropriate confidentiality and where they can express vulnerability without it seeming to be condemned as weakness. We live at a time when many shades and hues of congregation are experiencing numerical growth. In many cases, this is due to very good local leadership. On occasion it is not always easy for new and old members to see the need for excessive loyalty to a historic tradition and to external leaders who are its guardians and exemplars. Similarly, senior leaders appointed from such traditions to preside over dioceses or more do not find it easy to relate to shades other than their own, and to tasks where representation and oversight of the whole is essential to their work. The danger of congregationalism is that it reacts against external leadership and oversight. The danger of inappropriate oversight is that it ceases to be effective in relation to the local congregation when it suggests an excessive authoritarianism reminiscent of a past age. The rediscovery of a renewed loyalty and mutuality within *episkope* can provide a bridge between these tendencies.

Without this timely and urgent exploration, the tensions between national and local leaders will increase. The questions are strong and clear. Their answers require a relearning of the nature of leadership and oversight in episcopal churches; when are bishops leaders; who are the real leaders; where does power reside; is oversight something different from leadership and why is more than local oversight part of the essence of episcopal churches? The examination of these questions and the answers which are emerging can, in my view, give value to our understandings of why we can continue to believe in and practise this old idea.

The 'machinery' of mystery

How churches work and how their different congregations, committees and councils fit together can seem to be quite a mystery even to the initiated and the experienced. Denominations which have been in existence for centuries have developed their own characteristics and distinctive way of operating. This is even more so with episcopal churches which take a pride in tracing their origins back to the first communities of Christians. With a time span of two thousand years, so many changes and adaptations have taken place that these complex organizations need ecclesiastical lawyers and experts in what is called ecclesiology to explain them.[2]

Because debates about the structure of the local congregation and the deployment of ministers are becoming an essential part of the mission and resource thinking of episcopal churches, it has become important for those who engage in these debates to know what kind of a church they are restructuring. There is a need, probably for the first time, to explain in some detail what episcopal churches are, why their leadership has emerged in the way that it has and how participation in its life takes place. Some of the practices and procedures are different from those in other organizations and the reasons for this have to be explored and explained in more public ways. Members of episcopal churches and their leaders need to know why they belong to and value their tradition and what it is about the shape and structure of this Church that, in however distorted and adapted ways, still makes it a place where the excitement of knowing about faith in Jesus Christ can be experienced.

In a wise reflection on the essence of Anglican episcopal churches, Paul Avis says, 'Anglicanism believes that it embodies a dispersed authority that is compatible with much diversity in belief and practice'.[3] Such a well-balanced statement both describes what unites the international Anglican Communion and what has the potential to attack and divide it. Contained within such a statement are all the challenges which those appointed to leadership in Anglican churches face today. What does dispersed authority look like? How much diversity of belief can be contained? Can authority dictate practice or does diversity of practice demonstrate a tolerant and inclusive Anglican maturity?

One of the most significant recent reports about the nature and structure of the Church of England is called *Working as One Body* and is the product of an Archbishops Commission chaired by the Rt Rev Michael Turnbull who at the time was Bishop of Durham.[4] Many of the recommendations have been taken up and situations addressed. Other stated issues have become if anything worse than described in that 1995 report. Much of what is said in the introduction of the report can apply to any historic denomination and especially to episcopal churches today:

> The constituent bodies of the Church of England form part of an inherently complex whole. They are the natural outcome of a

long history of piecemeal development. Much of what goes on at
the national level puzzles and dismays many in the parishes and
the dioceses, who wonder how much confidence they can have in
the central organization of the church.[5]

For most of the time members of congregations do not have to
think about how their church works or trouble themselves about
where accountability rests. It is only when a transition of some
kind takes place or when a crisis occurs that they become aware
of belonging to something much bigger than the local. A change
of minister brings to the parish and congregation a bishop or
an archdeacon and even a patron, all of whom have a significant
part to play in the next appointment. The need to be aware of the
wider structure of an episcopal church becomes even greater when
proposals emerge to amalgamate parishes and change the way in
which clergy are deployed. Many new Christians, used to secular
appointment practices, find themselves on a steep learning curve.
Others who have begun life as members of a non-episcopal denomination ask questions about why the local does not predominate in
decision-making processes.

Episcopacy and the Body of Christ

Episcopally structured churches and their local congregations are
organically joined as parts of one whole – what St Paul called the
Body of Christ. The body is held together and given meaning and
reality primarily through the concept and practice of the ministry of
bishops. The binding cement which holds the two parts together is
mutual consent and respect. The bishop is represented locally by the
priest and congregation and the bishop is only effective and credible
in office if their representative ministry arises from and is acknowledged by the life and worship of the local congregation. This is a
particular way of saying that *episkope* has a great amount of mutuality
in its essential make-up. While the bishop 'looks over' (*epi-skope*) the

congregations and can usually see farther than them and where they need to go, so also congregations and all other church agencies and officers share in one mutual concept of 'overseeing' and caring for one another. Difference is held within an underlying commitment to unity and an understanding that diversity adds to the richness of one single ecclesiastical tradition.

There are many outstanding studies of what works and what does not work in the life of local congregations. We know a great deal about how to run small, medium-sized and large congregations, we are learning about local ministry exercised in teams or collaborative groups and we are overwhelmed by the imperative that all must be encompassed in the desire to share faith in appropriate methods of Christian mission and pioneer ministry. Sophistication in understanding the nuances and foibles of work in the local church is essential. This may well not be the overarching ingredient in 'Free' or 'Reformed' churches and in many 'House Church' structures. If such local or independent understandings are thought to be *all* that is necessary in episcopally led churches then a serious omission or misunderstanding is occurring.

Churches with episcopal leadership and the structures which stem from it do not have the luxury or option to be congregations which opt out or behave as if they were independent, or only loosely connected to their denomination. The strength of belonging to an organization larger than the local church is that it connects the congregation and its minister to a system which provides scrutiny, protection, accountability and identity. These benefits are clear for the local church and have to be exemplified in the practice of senior leaders if they are to play a respected part in the exercise of leadership.

The landmark report which looked at episcopacy and the work of bishops in modern times was produced by a group commissioned by the Archbishops of Canterbury and York with Chancellor Sheila Cameron QC as its chair. This 1980 report called *Episcopal Ministry*[6] could have laid the foundations for much work on *episkope*, but its membership found agreement hard to reach and events in the world church concerning the ordination of women as priests and a first woman in the United States consecrated as a bishop put pressure on it to reach conclusions and make recommendations. In practice the report is comprehensive in its historical sweep and detailed in its descriptions of other episcopal churches. It lists and places in context, rather than explores, ecumenical agreements concerning episcopal ministry without making significant theological connections. Most interesting of all, the report contains a dissenting view by Rev Dr George Carey who at the time was Principal of Trinity Theological College in Bristol and who in 1991 became Archbishop of Canterbury. Part of his concern was for more biblical work to be done and for this to lead to a deeper examination of whether 'maleness' or 'humanity' are the essence of the leadership expressed in an episcopal ministry derived from the apostles and representing Christ himself. The argument continues to this day, and continues to divide episcopal churches.

Significantly for this study, the Cameron Report sets out at an early stage to underline that oversight (*episkope*) is a gift from God for the church and is no human organizational convenience. Speaking about the origins of the ministry of oversight in the early church the report says:

> An essential principle which remains constant from the start, through all the variations of form, is that the ministry of oversight is not a human invention but a gift of God to the Church. It is a gift of guardianship of faith and order, enabling the Church to carry on the ministry of Jesus and to become what God intends, in mission, unity and holiness. It is God's creative act within the young Church to bring into being and to sustain a pastoral office in which an image of its own nature can be seen, and in which and by which He points to the nature of the Church itself.[7]

This early quotation provides the foundation as well as a justification for our further exploration. It allows us to expand and value the richness of what oversight can look like in a newly worked out theology and practice of *episkope*. It will link us to the necessary understandings of leadership, but more than that, it will enable us to discover or rediscover the basic concept within the ministry of the Church that unites and forms a basis for unity that is stronger and more fundamental than the divisions in practice, which it seems will always challenge a growing and developing church.

Leadership as oversight

Before we engage with the ways in which *episkope* is being used as a model to encompass both leadership and oversight, we need to look at a definition of leadership itself. From that we then have to ask whether leadership in episcopal churches has to be of a particular kind and have any significantly different characteristics from those of any other organization. That exploration will take us on to see why the concept of oversight is essential as a way of exercising leadership in the ways in which episcopal churches have come to be structured. The roots of the word come from the Old English *laedan*, which has meanings and uses such as travelling together and making pathways through to a new place. It comes from ideas and concepts of people using their inner resources and joint efforts and collective wisdom to develop their lives. In modern terms, leadership is concerned with ways of creating and achieving a desired future. Team leadership joins ancient and new definitions together because it talks about people making a journey together. That means staying focused on the future, as wisdom and tasks are shared in good times and when the going is tough.

Most of the things which can be said about leadership and oversight in large 'not for profit' or voluntary organizations can also be said about the structure, organization and leadership of churches. Styles and structures may differ for historic or doctrinal reasons or simply because congregations are new and at a particular stage in their life cycle.[8] In similar ways, leadership in its exercise and structure has different manifestations in the communities of world faiths. Structures and concepts differ according to the history, culture and values of the places where a faith had its origins.

However, to think of a bishop's work as the equivalent to that of a CEO (Chief Executive Officer) would be a great mistake. Many who telephone the bishop's office or who write in with complaints expect executive action of this kind. Many CEOs would say that exactly the same misunderstandings occur about the range of sanctions they can apply. Churches have a great mix of paid and voluntary members, and different approaches to authority are needed. How, then, are we to think of bishops and their responsibility for oversight and governance in the face of pressure from outside and from within to make them just like a CEO? The first step has to be to analyse the kind of organization an episcopal church is. Only after that can the different roles and responsibilities be understood in relation to all those who form the senior leadership. Episcopal churches are dispersed networks with accountability residing in a number of different places. Bishops have a series of roles to fulfil. Some of these are executive, some are pastoral and some are disciplinary. None are completely clear-cut, and they cannot be understood without a certain comprehension of how this broadly based organization with a hierarchy and with a consultative, sometimes legislative synodical framework actually works. Now is the time to describe and reform how it works.

Can *episkope* be the new, old idea?

There are two studies to be done: one is for the historic churches with bishops as their senior leaders, and the other is for the churches of the Reformation and beyond which do not have bishops in the hierarchical sense, but whose structures of government and account-ability have a different philosophy. The chapters which follow will be about leadership and oversight in episcopally structured churches. They will explore the tensions and examine ways for new

interpretations of *episkope* that will give new life to an old and fundamental concept. The added importance of such a study is that it is
not and cannot only be about helping those appointed to high office
to 'be a better bishop', though I hope that it will help in this sphere.
It will primarily be about the ways in which the work of *episkope* can
be valued and shared in a renewed way. As the title of this chapter
suggests – *episkope* can become a new old idea!

I have become convinced that such a broadened understanding
of the sharing of responsible leadership in churches with a tradition
of being led by bishops is possible. Leadership and oversight might
seem deceptively clear-cut in their application to the work of the
bishop and the staff members who work with them – archdeacons,
the cathedral dean, the diocesan secretary and principal specialist
officers. The expansion or rediscovery of shared *episkope* will show
that the outworking or interpretation of what in some places has
come to be an unnecessarily narrow concept is capable of rich
expansion and reinterpretation.

New thinking about *episkope*

Two of the most valued and influential thinkers and writers on
ministry in recent years, Steven Croft and Robin Greenwood, have
come to see that *episkope* is an essential concept in the teaching,
leadership and oversight of God's people which is exercised locally
as well as by senior leaders at the top of a denomination. Their work
has made a beginning in rehabilitating a concept which has become
distorted. It is interesting that, as far as I have been able to observe,
it is the parts of their writing which deal with matters other than
episkope which have received the most attention.

Croft's book *Ministry in Three Dimensions* has been very influential
for many in bringing traditional understandings of ministry to bear
upon the missionary demands of the contemporary church.[9] The
final section of his book is devoted to *episkope* in the local church,
which he calls 'enabling the ministry of others'. It has received less

attention, perhaps because it tiptoes into sensitive territory which has become the overstated role of one other particular group. He describes well for us the fundamental basis for shared *episkope* in the churches. With a wide-ranging scriptural review, he sets out how he understands God to work through the characters and personalities, prophets, judges, kings and many ordinary women and men in the books of the Bible. He underpins this with a theology which looks at the developed concept of God as Trinity – three persons working together to begin and continue what he calls 'the great dramas of creation and redemption'. The book is very appropriately focused on life and growth in local churches. It does not address the major issue of the exercise of shared *episkope* in senior positions. Now that Croft himself is a diocesan bishop, perhaps we can look forward to another book developing this theme?

One of the other significant writers on local church ministry, and also someone with an international reputation, is Robin Greenwood. In his most recent book *Parish Priests: for the sake of the Kingdom* he has also begun to explore the concept of *episkope* as a fundamental part of the understanding of the life of the church at its local and congregational levels.[10] Where Croft writes from the standpoint of the evangelist and missioner, Greenwood writes as someone formed by the Parish Communion movement and approaches *episkope* from a more eucharistically based theological position.

Like Steven Croft, Robin Greenwood is sure that the first place that *episkope* should be exercised and experienced is in the local church or congregation. Greenwood develops a theology that looks at the way in which congregations worship if they have as their main focus the Holy Communion or Eucharist service. Here, with many forms of liturgical renewal, there are visible signs of participation – the altar moved forward so that the priest or 'president' faces the people and 'presides' – with much active participation from lay people and other ministers. Greenwood rehabilitates the concept that the priest presides over or 'oversees' the whole work of the eucharistic community. This is demonstrated most visibly in the regular celebration by that community of the Holy Communion. While the focus is on the local, Greenwood also looks forward to an understanding which has implications for the local or diocesan bishop:

> But there are implications here for how bishops, in the way they function and in their attitudes, might share the responsibility for lifting the Church into patterns which are interactive and foster *communion.*[11]

A new *episkope* for a new age

A series of questions about the nature of leadership in the Christian churches is emerging. Are there some essential ingredients which make the concept of *episkope* work as an overarching idea? What is it that makes this kind of governance continue and form the backbone of the largest of our historic denominations? The focus on episcopal leadership arising from studies of local and regional leadership is essential and timely. Episcopal leadership is not about 'command and control' or about the creation or perpetuation of a 'ruling class' among church leaders. Episcopal leadership arises from the authority given to it by the members of congregations and from clergy or ministers. Such authority has special characteristics because it is given after thought and prayer by those who appoint church leaders for our age. The divine legitimation of the office by ordination – the laying on of hands – by other bishops emphasizes the corporate nature of the responsibility as well as the particular divine commission which 'sets apart' this recognized leadership role for necessary and understood tasks in a wider or 'universal' church. What these tasks are and what the modern roles should be is the challenging exploration which is being undertaken in the chapters that follow. Leadership and oversight are not new words, but a studied application of them placed together for episcopal churches may bear new fruit and help in the particular times of difficulty and even of crisis which surround the appointment and authority of episcopal leaders in many parts of the world.

As we begin this study, many basic questions leap out and ideas suggest themselves as possible alternative ways of running a church. There is one basic challenge in particular. Do we value *episkope* enough to want to continue with it as the core unifying characteristic of our church? If we do want a renewed sense of *episkope* in a church with bishops as the senior representative people, do we want them to exercise their office in different ways? In many of the episcopally led churches the work of bishops is already under examination. How do they share responsibilities with their staff and synodical colleagues? They have a central place in the life of their churches and are fundamental to its life and structure. But what bishops do and the function they fill has changed dramatically through the centuries. They have moved from being the nominated or elected senior minister in a town or region to becoming aristocratic princes with palaces and lands and a voice in the government of their nation. Modern bishops are halfway back to being appointed by the members of their churches and to being part of the conscience of a nation rather than a part of its ruling elite But bishops and those who share their episcopal ministry are expensive and they have to exemplify the best of what their denomination holds dear. If they are to remain, then they have to justify their place in our churches and in the wider society where they also operate. Some of this they can do for themselves; much more will be done for them by the context in which they work. A rigorous reappraisal is needed, not just of the work of bishops but of how governance is exercised in episcopal churches, and that is what this book sets out to do.

Episkope and accountability

In any kind of organization we want our leaders to be of the highest quality, we want them to have the essential skills of competence and effectiveness; but we also want them to be personable, people of integrity with the ability to motivate and inspire many others. They need to give oversight without being overbearing. Set against those high expectations we also know that leaders can all too often fall short even of their own ideals. They become more and more compromised as difficult decisions are made, and fall from their pedestals built on hope and expectation. We discover that, talented as most are in human terms, they are as fallible as the rest of us. When held publicly accountable, their faults and weaknesses are all too easily, even if necessarily, revealed. So it is that trust and accountability are among the most important elements in any modern organization and this has to be exemplified in its leaders. Churches and faith groups have to be subject to the same credibility test. The place of the church leader is exceptionally significant because religions by their very nature hold views and make statements about public life and private morality that can attempt to influence the whole of a society. As a very appropriate consequence, the leaders of such organizations come under particular scrutiny. Their life and character have to epitomize high moral values as they set the tone for the part of a world faith which they represent. Today, those values, held with integrity, can still be controversial and provoke disagreement even within their own denomination. Their public statements and private lifestyle can come under the media spotlight, and on occasions they can be as open to scrutiny and public interest as any pop star or celebrity footballer.

When things go wrong, accountability and transparency are expected. Fallible human leaders can show a certain amount of vulnerability and inadequacy but if a boundary is crossed and weakness turns into corruption or self-gratification then the penalties which are the other face of privilege come into play. In the structures of our churches, public scrutiny and a process where the accused are examined and held to account in a just way is very important. There have been times when such scrutiny and accountability has been difficult to achieve. Confidentiality of appointment and a preference for internal disciplinary procedures which mask effectiveness have been the practice for centuries. On occasions the inadequate and the wrongdoer have been supported for all too long without being brought to account. The potential embarrassment of high moral codes being breached has led to procrastination and on occasion an undermining of confidence in the whole institution. The controversies surrounding alleged child abuse in schools and care homes run by a diocese or religious order are but one example causing great difficulty in many countries. Clarity of what we need and expect from our leaders has to be the primary measure for the assessment of success or failure. Not to know how to intervene or when to sense that things are going wrong is a failure we can attribute to the structure of a church as much as to the activities of its individual leaders. It is a part of governance appropriately expressed as *episkope*.

The need for a clarity of purpose

Christianity needs to become more robust in its exercise of appropriate leadership for other reasons than having similar characteristics to other large organizations. It needs to demonstrate the value of leadership and oversight exercised in this particular way. This can only be achieved when there is a much greater clarity of purpose for the church which holds this form of leadership as essential to its nature. We are in a completely new situation where the faiths of the world have achieved prominence by being associated with conflicts and events which might not altogether be good. Christianity is now seen much more widely than ever before as one faith among many. All faith leaders need to be able to calm inflamed situations in many parts of the world where religion is a cultural factor in a conflict. Faith leaders need to equip migrants and settlers for new lives in countries where the culture and traditions of their faith do not sit easily with the norms and even the values of the host country. They need to interpret the faith which they represent to leaders of other faiths, to political regimes and to a media which may well appear to be hostile. Most significantly for this study, Christian leaders from episcopally led and governed churches need to know and understand how other faiths and traditions understand and value their leadership. Rarely can one faith leader speak for all others and command support. Bishops themselves are one faith and denominational leader among several, each exercising oversight over the same territory.

One of the best studies of Anglicanism is by Professor and Bishop Stephen Sykes. In his *The Integrity of Anglicanism* he describes a church which has bishops as a core part of its understanding. But he says that our Anglican bishops in most places around the world are one bishop among many representing local episcopal leadership in different parts of a 'broken' church. If this is the case, and if Anglicanism has a distinct understanding of its own use of *episkope*, then it is important for us to set out together with other members of the broken body on these new explorations. We can even say that we are attempting, for the benefit of the whole Church, to answer a question which Sykes poses towards the end of his book:

> And at the very least one imagines it would be helpful to today's bishops in the Anglican communion to discover what their vocation is in a broken church, and what its relation is to the true church.[12]

Boldness is needed to grasp a future where religion has a new significance. One of the strengths of episcopal churches is that their core values arise from a strong belief both in the adaptability and development of their tradition and also in a continuity of structure and belief. The greatest strength is in their ability to reinterpret and change around non-negotiable fundamental concepts. One of these is the office of bishop as the leader within a corporate sharing in *episkope* which derives authority and continuity in a historic succession from the apostles themselves.

Even at this early stage in our investigation we can see that the concept of *episkope* which was used in the early centuries as the means of governance in the churches is one which will allow a great deal of development. Some of its reinterpretation could serve as illustration and example for commercial companies, the voluntary sector and for some aspects of school and health care management, all complex organizations struggling with change and innovation. Leadership and oversight are the key ingredients of effective working in any organization. In particular, creativity and 'new life' are part and parcel of the values and the foundation of the faith we share. By its very nature Christianity has the ability to understand itself in new ways and to show resurrection life. The identification and testing of new models for leadership and oversight as a redefined combination of working practices known as *episkope* make this an exciting and challenging idea. It could help us to believe again in the church which has formed us and given us the ability and the permission to explore searching questions. This concept which has inspired and created a church has become distorted and not as fit for purpose as it might be. In the next chapter I want to look at where episcopal leadership has come from and how it has been forged and shaped on the anvil of history.

Notes

1 Mantle, Jonathan, *Archbishop: the life and times of Robert Runcie*, Sinclair-Stevenson, 1991, pp. 73–4.

2 For a wider working out of Anglicanism within the family of episcopal churches, see a series of essays by Dr Colin Podmore, *Aspects of Anglican Identity*, Church House Publishing, 2005.

3 Avis, Paul, *Authority, Leadership and Conflict in the Church*, Mowbray (Continuum) 1992.

4 *Working as One Body* The Report of the Archbishops' Commission on the Organization of the Church of England. Church House Publishing, 1995.

5 *Working as One Body*, p. 24 para. 3.3.

6 *Episcopal Ministry*: The Report of the Archbishops' Commission on The Episcopate, Church House Publishing, 1990 GS Misc. 944.

7 op. cit. p. 17, para. v.37.

8 See the analyses and descriptions of congregations published by the Alban Institute, www.alban.org

9 Croft, Steven, *Ministry in three dimensions: ordination and leadership in the local church*, DLT, 1999.

10 Greenwood, Robin, *Parish Priests: for the sake of the Kingdom*, SPCK, 2009.

11 op. cit. p. 91.

12 Sykes Stephen, *The Integrity of Anglicanism*, Mowbray, 1978, p. 99.

III

Bishops old and new

Bishops are the principal exemplar of the overall exercise of *episkope*. They are far from being all that *episkope* expresses or requires, but they do represent a church in which through the centuries they have been the leaders. It is to the bishop as a person as well as a church office holder with certain specific responsibilities that much attention is given, and from whom much is expected. In looking at captivating images of bishops I have been particularly energized by an extended metaphor used by Donald Messer in *Contemporary images of Christian Ministry*. He gives his chapter on bishops the title 'Enslaved Liberators of the Rainbow Church'.[1] This very graphic description of the role and opportunities for leadership and oversight offered to a modern bishop encapsulates and suggests much. It tells us that there are constraints placed upon bishops by their role and from the inheritance of history. It tells us also that there are tremendous leadership possibilities open to bishops, but in a church which is very different from the one which formed the original episcopal model.

Where do bishops come from?

Leadership and oversight mean particular things in Christian communities, and to find their origins we have to look again at the beginnings of the church and the first Christian uses of the word *episkope*. There are no bishops in the four gospels, nor is there any account of Jesus ordaining people directly with the title of priest or bishop. What we have is Jesus calling people to be his disciples, training them in his thought and ideas and sending them out as 'apostles'. This is the first word used for those with a special commission to preach and teach and to lead others in ministry.

In the New Testament, the early Christian congregations began to develop a system of order for themselves. There was a leader or chief presbyter in each congregation and, so it seems, one of these was appointed or elected as the senior of all the presbyters in a town or community. The role was one of 'oversight' and carried some authority to teach and to guard the tradition of faith which was being passed on or transmitted from the first disciples and apostles of Jesus. In Peter's farewell speech to the Ephesian elders in Acts 20.28, he says that the Holy Spirit has placed them to be overseers (*episkopous*) and shepherds of the church. For most of the time in the New Testament all *presbuteroi* are *episkopoi*. The only other use is of Jesus himself and that is in I Peter 2.25. 'For you were straying like sheep, but have now returned to the shepherd and guardian (*episkopon*) of your souls.'

The New Testament does not describe a single pattern of ministry which might serve as a blueprint for any or all future ministry in the church. There may well have been a variety of tasks requiring different forms of leadership existing in different places. As the work of spreading the gospel developed and local worshipping communities became established, certain elements from early practice were developed into a more common pattern of ministry. The words 'presbyter' and 'bishop' were not used for itinerant charismatics and preachers but for leaders of settled congregations. There were local ministries of presbyter-bishops and of deacons, and a general ministry of apostles and prophets. It was not until early in the second century that the threefold ministry of bishop, presbyter and deacon emerged and had universal use.[2] Character and integrity of lifestyle were very important indeed. In the Epistle of Titus, one of the Pastoral Epistles, there is the interchangeable use of presbyter and bishop:

> That is why I left you in Crete, that you might amend what was defective, and appoint elders (*presbuterous*) in every town as I directed you (v5) ... For a bishop (*episkopon*), as God's steward, must be blameless, not quick tempered or arrogant or a drunkard or violent or greedy for gain, but hospitable, a lover of goodness, master of himself, upright, holy, and self-controlled. He must hold firm to the sure word as taught, so that he may be able to give instruction in sound doctrine and also to confute those who contradict it (v7–9).

There was a gradual development of the office and function of leaders as new thresholds were crossed and broader organization was needed. In place of the early designations 'those who labour among you' (I Thess. 5.12) or 'fellow workers' (I Cor. 16.16) 'your leaders' appears (Heb. 13.17). Then we see more formal descriptions: 'elders' and *episkopoi* with *diakonoi* as assistants with specific community roles begin to appear. Presbyters and *episkopoi*/overseers seem to be interchangeable titles, but we cannot tell if there were different duties for each. One view is that the titles were the same and it was not until there became more intercommunication between congregations that the difference was noticed.[2] A significant distinction in meaning between the two titles only developed when the separated episcopate began to emerge. Then it was clear that the *episkopos* was chairman of the board of elders or head of the college of presbyters.

Ignatius of Antioch (martyred between 98 and 117) is the first to mention this development; as Ignatius was the successor but one to St Peter, the letters have particular significance. While being deported from Alexandria to Rome, Ignatius wrote letters to bishops of the churches along his way. In most places there was only one bishop for each community, but in Rome he wrote to a team of bishops who worked collectively.

It is clear from these letters and from other documents of a similar time that a distinct pattern was emerging. In the Didache (about 120) local officials are bishops and deacons. In the First Letter of Clement (96) which mentions only bishops and deacons, a single bishop was expected to lead or at least to be the president of a council of presbyters for the church in each geographical area. Deacons had by this time, and probably always, a more service-focused role in the local community. As the Church continued to expand, groups of congregations in cities and townships elected their own *episkopos*, whereas churches in the regions around an important city were most likely to be served by presbyters and deacons from the bishop's city church. Thus, in time, the bishop changed from being the leader of a single church confined to an urban area to being the leader of the churches of a given geographical area. The bishop's jurisdiction was always related, as today, to the name of a place or specific geographical area.

Rudolph Bultmann explores the significant ecclesiological issue of how, at this stage in its life, the church began to understand itself. It was becoming much more than an association of local congregations, each with their own bishop. The concept of a 'Church' with a structure and wider organization was beginning to emerge.

His view is that, from the letters of Clement, the predominant view of the early church by around 100 was that Jesus Christ was anointed and commissioned by God. Jesus himself commissioned the apostles. They then spread the gospel proclamation through lands and cities, everywhere appointing presbyters/bishops and deacons, and arranged for them to appoint their successors. Bultmann says:

> The decisive step has then been taken: henceforth the office is regarded as *constitutive of the Church*. The whole church rests upon

the office-bearers, whose office is held to go back in uninter-
rupted succession to the apostles.... The Spirit is henceforth
bound to the office and is transmitted by a sacramental act,
ordination by the laying on of hands (Acts 6.6, 13.3, I Tim. 4.14,
II Tim. 1.6 and possibly II Tim. 5.22).[3]

In this sensitive description of the structure of life in the early Church
drawn from the scriptures and the Church Fathers, Bultmann sets
out a view which also provides scope for interpretation and which
has fed the reform of churches through the centuries. Interpretations
continue to give opportunity for controversy and renewal today.
As church structures and ecclesiastical organization has developed
through the centuries, it is the human face of the work of a bishop
which has made them so significant in the history of a church and
in the controversies which are inherent in the development of the
modern nation state.

The bishop as servant and shepherd

The first great bishop administrator was Pope Gregory the Great
(c.540–604). He saw the need to Christianize Britain and sent
the Benedictine monk Augustine to lead a mission to convert the
king and kingdom of Kent. It was Gregory who provided one of
the great models for bishops as well as for priests. He said that a
bishop was always to be 'the servant of the servants of God'. He
wrote the first handbook about being a bishop. It is called the *Liber
Regulae Pastoralis* and is known as the *Pastoral Rule*. The book was
written soon after Gregory became Pope in 590, and was addressed
to the Bishop of Ravenna, in reply to inquiries received from him
respecting the duties and obligations of the clergy.

About the work and duties of a bishop he says:

The conduct of a bishop ought so far to be superior to the
conduct of the people as the life of a shepherd is accustomed to
exalt him above the flock. For one whose position is such that the

people are called his flock ought anxiously to consider how great a necessity is laid upon him to maintain uprightness. It is necessary, then, that in thought he should be pure, in action firm; discreet in keeping silence; profitable in speech; a near neighbor to every one in sympathy; exalted above all in contemplation; a familiar friend of good livers through humility, unbending against the vices of evil-doers through zeal for righteousness; not relaxing in his care for what is inward by reason of being occupied in outward things, nor neglecting to provide for outward things in his anxiety for what is inward.[4]

This is indeed a counsel of perfection and one which, though ideal in its ambition, one to which no human being can do more than aspire. Many bishops have earned a place in history though failing to come near to such a high calling, while a few remain an inspiration because they not only represent these values and qualities in themselves but have also been able to inspire dedication and imitation in others.

To describe a bishop as a servant or as a shepherd is to give an immediate picture in the mind's eye. It suggests that the role is always in relationship with others and that there are differing types or models for the ways in which being a bishop can be described. For the former there is almost universal agreement, for the latter there are many different views and interpretations. Much of what differs and what can be contentious comes from the range of ways in which bishops have used and abused their role. How much the culture informs and shapes the work of a bishop, and how much a bishop can stand out against the prevailing attitudes and structures of a society, is one of the challenging paradoxes of ecclesiastical history.

The bishop as monarch

The development of both social and theological understandings of ministries of oversight exercised by people who were by the end of the first century called bishops is important. In the succeeding centuries bishops became less and less people who emerged as the leaders of local groups of presbyters or even missioners to other lands. New bishops were people appointed by existing bishops who consecrated them by the laying on of hands. As bishops became part of the groups who were the rulers in regions, they became separated from the local clergy and congregations who had originally been the people who appointed them. They were chosen from groups who were part of the ruling élite and developed a way of exercising their office and authority in a distinctive and separated way.

Gradually bishops became a self-appointing and self-perpetuating class, and one of the groups who ruled European society. Such a development does not mean that their theological, teaching and pastoral roles became less necessary or valued, but that their life and much of their work was separated from the immediate ministry of local churches. The concept of 'monarchical episcopacy' emerged to describe this aristocratic and more distanced role. The most godly and the most able were needed to be teachers and guardians of the faith. The position, influence and wealth which accompanied the office produced many problems. Corrupt practice can be an easy temptation as the trappings of worldly power and wealth increase.

The bishop as missionary

In spite of the locally appointed nature of early bishops, many have become missionaries and travelled widely. In contrast to the trappings of the king's court and the compromises of wealth, many bishops, often with origins in the religious orders, were those who engaged in missionary activity. They were bold pioneers. By their status and position missionary bishops were able to gain access to kings and local leaders either to convert them or to get consent for the tribe or nation to become Christian.

Columba (521–597) was an Irish monk who became a missionary to the Picts in southern Scotland and is particularly associated with Iona. Augustine of Canterbury was sent from Rome to be Archbishop and given authority over the British bishops by Pope Gregory the Great. He landed in 597 and was instrumental in the conversion of Kent, but his authority was rejected by the British monks and bishops. His original intention was to establish an archbishopric in London, but this ignored the political fact that London was in the realm of decidedly pagan tribes, so Canterbury, the capital of the Kentish kingdom, became the seat of the pre-eminent archbishop in England.

Ansgar was a Benedictine monk of Saxon family, born in Corbie, France in 801. In 826, when King Harald of Denmark asked for missionaries, Ansgar led a group to Denmark, and a few years later to Sweden. Because of unsettled political conditions, his work ran into difficulties and Ansgar withdrew into Germany where he served as first Archbishop of Hamburg and then of Bremen. Later, however, he helped to consecrate Gotbert the first bishop of Sweden. He led missionary activity in Denmark and in Sweden and has earned the reverential title 'Apostle to the North'.

Such missionary bishops mark one kind of leader. Their efforts are replicated through the centuries and find echoes in the missionary bishops who followed their empire building nations to the colonies in the greater part of the nineteenth and into the twentieth centuries. They are in marked contrast to the bishops who were appointed by rulers as they conquered the nations of Europe.

The bishop as baron

It is easy to get lost in the tangles of history but for the next sections of our story it is necessary to explore how the church and its bishops became so closely associated with their king, prince and the affairs of state. Europe in the Middle Ages and at the time of the Renaissance had bishops, and Rome had popes, who were surrounded by wealth. The pastoral contact between the bishops and dioceses carved out of the former Roman Empire gradually became lost. Diocesan bishops in effect became feudal lords. The episcopal palaces across Europe were filled with aristocrats and party officials who had been rewarded by their king or prince for their work and support. A.G. Dickens describes the route to preferment:

> Apart from high birth, a doctorate in the civil law, followed by a few ambassadorial missions or a few years in chancery, was a far surer road to high preferment than sanctity of character, eminence in sacred learning, missionary activities or even ecclesiastical administration.... At every level it was accepted that office holders should draw their stipends and hire working deputies at much lower rates.[5]

Bishops in the Middle Ages hardly conformed to the model of 'servant of the servants'. Once appointed and consecrated, they would make a primary visitation to their parishes to make sure that the clergy were properly licensed and that they were legally entitled to their benefits. Having done this the bishop would often retreat to a palace away from the diocese and within easy reach of his prince and the court. Here he would give his time to matters of state and to administering his lands. The model is more one of a feudal baron and prince of the church. Diocesan matters were at first left to archdeacons and to relatively impoverished suffragan bishops. Gradually, matters were taken over by the bishop's legal officers and the chancery. The contact of clergy and congregations with their diocesan bishop was as the administrator of discipline rather than in any way a pastoral one. The clergy remained in their parishes cultivating their land as they had done for centuries. Churchwardens were prominent local figures, responsible for accounts and the administration of lands left for the upkeep of the church.[6]

One of our twentieth century theologians, looking at the development of leadership structures in the early centuries, does not see the emergence of monarchical episcopacy as a good thing at all. The German theologian Jürgen Moltmann is a strident critic:

> The growth of the monarchical episcopate broke up the genetic relationship between the commissioned church and its special

commissions in a way that was totally one-sided. The aristocratic justification of the ministry of a 'vénérable compagnie des pasteurs' – a group that reproduces itself through co-optation and only recognizes brotherhood on the level of 'brothers in office' – can hardly be judged as progress, qualitatively speaking.[7]

The bishop as politician

The story of the relationship between church and state has different characteristics in every country of the world. Nowadays we also have to take into account the relationship to the state of other faiths. This differs considerably in many places. One of the challenges in modern life is that of accommodating any historic religion to the assumptions and political interventions of a national government. It is the individual church member who has to follow their conscience as many new pieces of legislation are brought in, some of which do conflict with the teachings of a faith and of a national church. Local religious leaders have to give guidance and advice on many of these moral issues. They in turn are advised and guided by the national leaders of a religion. It is often the national religious leaders who have to conduct the negotiations with their governments. Through the centuries some have paid a heavy price for their opposition to some changes, while others owe their elevation to their reforming ideas and the needs of a monarch or state. This story is not a new one and it may be helpful to trace the origin of the relationship between a church and its national context in one particular country. The story of what happened in England is very accessible and contains lessons and warnings which are relevant in many places.

In 1017 most of England became a province of the Danish empire of King Canute. Danish rule continued until 1042, when the English monarchy was restored but proved weak. The crown passed to Norman hands in the form of William the Conqueror after the famous Battle of Hastings in 1066. Unlike previous conquests, the vast majority of the people were neither destroyed nor displaced.

The Normans introduced the feudal system of lords, vassals and fiefs. Thus a strict hierarchy was established from King down to peasant. Soon most of the high ranking positions, including bishoprics, were occupied by Normans.

At the time of Henry I (1068–1135) there were disputes over whether foreign bishops should swear loyalty to the Crown of England. Though a compromise was reached it required that every English bishop accept the Pope as overlord, thus the English church became fully subject to Rome and its authority. In the mid twelfth century the dispute about where authority over the church resided came to a head over the issue of whether clergy should be subject to civil law or not. These tensions are known well in English history and are marked in drama and literature. Probably the best known example is the murder of Archbishop Thomas á Becket (1170) by four misguided knights, which tainted the later years of the reign of Henry II.

The early years of the thirteenth century saw the dispute escalate with the refusal of King John to allow the papally appointed Archbishop of Canterbury into England. In response, in 1208 the Pope put England under interdict so that no church services were held and people were buried in unconsecrated ground without a service. This lasted until 1212 when the Pope declared Philip of France to be King of England, and in response King John effectively surrendered his crown to the Pope and ruled as a vassal of the See of Rome with a large tribute to be paid every year.

Such disputes reflect the style and manner of the appointment of bishops which had become established in England. There was authority from the Pope and an ultimate acknowledgement that it was he who appointed bishops throughout Western Europe. But there was a growing tension between pope and king or local prince. There was also an emerging tension between clergy and lay people growing in wealth and influence, including significant churchmen and both pope and king. In particular the differences and tensions were reflected in laws which defined the boundaries and limits of mutual authority.

The Statute of Provisors (1306), passed in the reign of Edward I, enacted 'that no tax imposed by any religious persons should be sent out of the country whether under the name of a rent, tallage, tribute or any kind of imposition.' A much greater check on the freedom of action of the popes was imposed by the later Statute of Provisors (1351), which said that the election of bishops 'should be free'. The Statute of Praemunire of 1352–3 was the foundation of much legislation preventing taxes and tithes collected in England being passed to any 'foreign power', in this case the Pope in Rome. It was not finally repealed until the Criminal Law Act of 1967.

In England one interesting document gave energy to a growing sense that the monarch and the state should have independence from and authority over the church. The tract *Defensor Pacis* (The Defender of Peace) laid the foundations of modern doctrines of sovereignty. It was written by Marsilius of Padua, an Italian medieval scholar. It appeared in 1324 and provoked a storm of controversy that lasted through the century. The context of the work lies in the political struggle between Louis IV, the Holy Roman Emperor and Pope John XXII. The treatise is a vehemently anticlerical product of the secular and classicist thought that characterize Humanism. Marsilius' work was censured by Pope Benedict XII and Pope Clement VI.

Defensor Pacis extends the tradition of Dante's 'Monarchia', separating the secular state from religious authority. It affirmed the sovereignty of the people and civil law and sought to greatly limit the power of the Papacy, which he viewed as the 'cause of the trouble which prevails among men'. He proposed the seizure of church property by civil authority and the elimination of tithes.

As its name implies, it describes the state as the defender of the public peace. Marsilius denies, not only to the Pope, but also to the bishops and clergy, any coercive jurisdiction or any right to pronounce in temporal matters. Desiring to see the clergy practise a holy poverty, he proposes the suppression of tithes and the seizure by the secular power of the greater part of the property of the church.

The clergy, thus deprived of its wealth, privileges and jurisdiction, are further to be deprived of independence, for the civil power is to have the right of appointing to benefices, etc. The supreme authority in the church is to be the council, but a council summoned by the emperor.

The Pope was not to possess any more power than other bishops, though Marsilius recognizes that the supremacy of the See of Rome goes back to the earliest times of Christianity. He suggested that the Pope is to content himself with a pre-eminence mainly of an honorary kind, without claiming to interpret the Holy Scriptures, define dogmas or distribute benefices. Moreover, he is to be elected by the Christian people, or by the delegates of the people, the princes, or by the council, and these are also to have the power to punish, suspend or depose him. The theory contained a visionary plan of reformation which ended, not in the separation of the church from the state, but in the subjection of the church to the state. In 1535, Thomas Cromwell, Henry Vlll's Vicar General, paid a William Marshall to translate *Defensor Pacis* into English in order to give intellectual support to the implementation of Royal Supremacy.

By the mid thirteenth century, around one third of England was owned by monasteries, many livings were held by absentee foreign clergy and vast sums of money were leaving the country in the form of tithes. With this situation, backed by intellect and a desire for power and independence voiced by princes across Northern Europe, it is no surprise that reform began to be in the air. There were local revolts against oppressive monastic tithes and the excessive wealth which the church was accumulating around its bishoprics. There was a growing sense in many countries of Northern Europe that the bishops and the monasteries were draining rather than defending the faith.

The bishop as reformer

With such a background of unrest and dissatisfaction between local kings and princes and the papacy based in Rome, it is no surprise that when Henry VIII wanted a senior churchman to give him independence from Rome and champion the cause of his divorce, he remembered a note he had made years before after a chance meeting with a Cambridge don called Thomas Cranmer. A key source of dissent and debate for reform began in Cambridge with a group of academics who met in the White Horse Tavern to discuss the writings of the German monk and reformer Martin Luther. Among these were a group of future bishops and an archbishop: Thomas Cranmer, Matthew Parker, Hugh Latimer and Nicholas Ridley. Miles Coverdale, Robert Barnes, Prior of the Augustines and others who were to become Protestant Martyrs were also members of the group.

Henry had met Cranmer while staying at Waltham Abbey in 1529. He had heard the young don putting forward the idea that the matter of the legality of the king's marriage – and the possibility of an annulment – should be referred for an opinion to English academics and lawyers. When Archbishop Warham died in 1532 Henry remembered Cranmer and thought of him as someone who would be sympathetic to his cause and who would be willing to accept the divorce and sanction his marriage to the already pregnant Anne Boleyn. The child to be born had to be a legitimate child and heir. The method of appointing a bishop and an archbishop remained unchanged. Henry put forward Cranmer's name to the Pope, who consented, though with reservations about Cranmer's reforming views and associates.

It is normal for an Archbishop to be chosen from among the ranks of diocesan bishops but in this case, at the time the only contenders – Tunstall of Durham and Gardiner of Winchester – were too independent of spirit. Cranmer only held the sinecure of Archdeacon of Taunton. In 1533 Cranmer was consecrated bishop, having sworn an oath of loyalty to the Pope, which he said he intended not to consider as binding. He proceeded to the annulment of Henry's first marriage, the recognition of the marriage to Anne Boleyn and then to her Coronation. In 1534 the Act of Supremacy was passed.

One of the great chroniclers of the Middle Ages and of the way in which the monasteries were dissolved at the time of the Reformation is Professor Eamon Duffy. At the end of the turbulence of the fourteenth and fifteenth centuries he comments that what became the Church of England 'retained totally unchanged the full medieval framework of episcopal church government'.[8] By this he means that bishops were still appointed by the crown and their appointment ratified by the chapter of the cathedral to which they were appointed bishop. What had changed was that the monarch appointed bishops without reference to the Pope in Rome.

Of great interest at this reforming time, with so much influence of Protestantism from the Continent and with so much internal unrest in the nation, is that the concept of episcopacy survived, as did the method by which bishops were appointed. The oppressive influence of the Church and of the monasteries might have suggested the complete overthrow of a system. What happened was that the old ecclesiastical structures continued, but with the state in control of senior episcopal appointments.

To find the reason for this we have to look to the appointments of archbishop which Queen Elizabeth I made and to what is known as the 'Elizabethan Settlement'. Her three archbishops were Matthew Parker (1559–75), Edmund Grindal (1576–83) and John Whitgift (1583–1604). Each in their way were scholars and reformers, but with a strong sense of continuity. Parker and Grindal were influenced by Lutheranism which retained strong links with the state. In some of the Scandinavian countries it continued with not only an episcopal structure but also with an unreformed liturgy and the continued use of vestments and the Mass. Whitgift was a Calvinist and might well have wanted to take a different view of senior appointments, but was a supporter of episcopacy and of ordered worship through doctrines and regulations contained within the Book of Common Prayer of 1549.

Alongside this robust defence of episcopacy from a succession of Archbishops came support and an examination of episcopal ministry from Richard Hooker (1554–1600). His books *Of the Laws of Ecclesiastical Polity* put Hooker among a number of significant laypeople and clerics who, through their learning and piety, deepen an understanding of how a national church could be both spiritual and outgoing without undue compromise to its integrity. The poet priest George Herbert (1593–1633) gave a model of the devout and conscientious parish priest which influences many clergy and congregations today.

Hooker's writings (the later books may not have been authored by him) show the need to work out a balance in episcopal churches between the emerging European Protestant view of a commonality of belief and ministerial responsibility called 'the priesthood of all believers' and the place of those churches in nation states and in some countries where the monarch was also the head of the church. It is a debate which cascades down to this present day with tensions between synodical government and the collegial authority of bishops. The balance in church governance between what is called 'Conciliar' participative government and what is known and exercised by bishops and others as 'Magisterial' is one which has changed and which continues to change through the centuries.[9]

Elizabeth was succeeded by James VI of Scotland. He had seen the outworking of Scottish, Calvinist Presbyterianism and came with the attitude that further encouragement of Puritanism would not be right. His view was that Monarch and Episcopacy stood together. Consequently he entered into a close alliance with the established Church. He understood that he ruled by Divine Right and it was the duty of the Church to support him as he would support and encourage the Church. James called a conference at Hampton Court in 1604 to listen to the concerns of various church groups. He was heard to cry out during one discussion 'No Bishop, no King'. Only a short time later the whole country, under the Commonwealth of Oliver Cromwell, was to learn the opposite side of this – 'No King, no Bishops'.

Charles I, who became King of England in 1625, took the view of the Divine Right of Kings to an extreme and entered into a prolonged battle with parliament, which did not meet for eleven years after 1629. Without a parliament the earl of Stafford administered secular affairs on behalf of the King and to a large extent William Laud, Bishop of London and then Archbishop of Canterbury, did the same for the Church. Laud was a strong opponent of Calvinism and Puritanism throughout his career. He wanted to create a Chuch of England which was 'Catholic and Reformed'. Throughout the time of the Commonwealth, when no new bishops were appointed, Laud kept in close contact with the king in exile. He enforced high standards in the church as a form of defence, insisting that clergy and cathedral canons were resident and executed their office diligently. Laud was a dominant figure, autocratic as a reformer and as an enforcer – so much so that at a sitting of the House of Commons, Sir Edward Deering said, 'A Pope at Rome will do me less harm than a patriarch may doe at Lambeth'.[10] It was this kind of over-elevation of the role of bishop to become even more monarchical and prince-like which was so repulsive to many loyal members of the Church of England and strained their loyalty to breaking point. John Milton said that the church as he was experiencing it: 'new presbyter is but old priest writ large'. It was even more so with bishops who saw themselves at this time and after the Restoration more as prelates than as servants, pastors or shepherds of the flock. It was this re-invention of the role of bishop in the exercise of power and authority which led John Milton to decide against ordination and loyalty to his Church and which led him to say he had been 'church-outed by prelates'![11]

It was a natural consequence at the time of the Restoration to consider what kind of episcopal leadership would be re-established with the accession of Charles II in 1660. No new bishops had been appointed to sees during the Commonwealth. The situation was resolved by the Restoration before the situation became desperate. On the return of Charles as king there were moves by the Puritan party to establish a more moderate form of episcopacy, set out in a 1641 publication by Archbishop Usher, *Reduction of Episcopacy unto the Form of Synodical Government.* They were no match for the Laudian party which had kept his spirit and idea alive for more than fifteen years. The result was a return to the use of the Book of Common Prayer, the appointment of bishops by the monarch and a re-established and strong link between Church and King and now also with parliament. All this was agreed and enacted at the Savoy Conference of 1661.

The model of an intimate relationship between Church and State was re-established and consolidated. It was to remain the situation in England for centuries to come. Its unfortunate outcome was that episcopacy became corrupted by power and wealth and became increasingly separated from the life of diocese and parishes. Such a situation led to further moves for reform. The Wesleys led a renewal movement which eventually broke away from the Church of England, and reforming parties, High and Low, became a characteristic of church life. Significantly, Prime Ministers became more influential in the appointment of bishops than did the monarch. It is a situation which has remained almost to this present day.

Bishops as we know them today

It is to the mid-nineteenth century that we look. In the century or more before that, bishops were a secure part of the aristocracy of the nation. The Bishop of Oxford, Samuel Wilberforce (1805–73), is credited with beginning to create the modern shape of episcopal ministry. Before his time it was normal for the bishop to reside only infrequently in his diocese, to take little interest in its affairs and to delegate this work to his archdeacon. Wilberforce was Bishop of Oxford, resided there, visited his clergy and began a number of internal reforms and established Cuddesdon theological college. This new zeal and professionalism in bishops is seen also in the way clergy chose to perform their duties. Work was no longer left to poorly paid curates by absentee rectors but taken on by them in city, town and countryside alike. These moves towards an increasing professionalism have been well charted by Anthony Russell in his book *The Clerical Profession* and for reforming work in urban industrial areas by E.R. Wickham in *Church and People in an Industrial City*.

In modern times the work of a bishop has been subject to rigorous scrutiny. One of the main reasons for this has been the need for clarity of definition and role in discussions between different denominations and in the movement towards Christian Unity. In the discussions between the Church of England and the Methodist Church, the place of bishops was important, as the English Methodist Church has Superintendents and Chairmen. Equally the Nordic churches had to explore the nature of apostolic succession and the 'laying on of hands' in ordination, as consensus was reached in the Northern European discussion of recognition of ministries, called the Porvoo Agreement.

The bishop as authority figure

While not having the same role as a managing director in a company, a chief executive or a head teacher, bishops are the most senior people in all episcopally structured churches. They have great authority given to them by their church to exercise authority and discipline within their dioceses. It is a classic and particularly 'catholic' view that bishops are primarily the figure of authority in a diocese. Their status and their legal position confer on them certain rights and many responsibilities. In this sense they are not just senior priests among other priests but ones with particular responsibilities. They are responsible people called on by their church to exercise the authority and work of a bishop. These responsibilities are taken on with a due sense of humility and within the context of an overall *episkope*, a sense of obligation and responsibility for one another which is shared by all members of the church.

John Haliburton has set out his catholic understanding of bishops in an extended way in his book *The Authority of a Bishop*. He explores in some depth the question about where authority is located in the

Church of England and in the universal Catholic Church. He is clear that episcopal authority is a special thing and that it gains some of its authenticity through being able to trace its origins back to the early church. He is also clear that in a church with a hierarchical structure there is a particular place for bishops. He maintains his position not in order to distance bishops from other Christians but to place them in a definite way in the order and life of the Church:

> There is only one *episkope*, one ministry of oversight, exercised by the bishop and extended through those he appoints to the presbyteral order.[12]

This clear description explains well for us the relationship between a bishop and his clergy. In medieval churches and in many church sanctuaries today there is a bishop's chair. This symbolizes the very point that all ministry, whether in a diocese or in a parish, is a shared ministry. The charge which a bishop gives to a priest when placed in a parish is described as 'my charge and yours'.

The bishop as apostle

There is no doubt that the churches which have had bishops throughout their history regard the form of church order which bishops represent to be fundamental to their existence, and episcopal oversight essential to their structure. Much of the substance of the conversations between the Church of England and the Nordic Churches has centred around the need to prove that the appointment of their bishops comes in an unbroken chain from the appointment by St Peter of the first bishops. Equally, though perhaps of less inherent significance than was once thought, is the denial by the Roman Catholic Church of the validity of Anglican orders for doctrinal reasons as well as those of historical integrity.[13]

Michael Ramsey, theologian and archbishop, took a thorough look at the way in which bishops emerged as key figures in the life of the early church and in many different ways in the life of the church through the centuries. In his influential book, *The Gospel and the Catholic Church* he concluded:

> What matters most is not the opinions of English divines about Episcopacy, but the fact of its existence in the English church, just as what mattered in the first century was not the Corinthian's language nor even St Paul's language about his apostleship, but the fact that, under God, it existed. For its existence declared the truth that the church in England was not a new foundation nor a local realization of the invisible Church, but the expression on English soil of the one historical and continuous visible Church of God.[14]

The bishop as enslaved liberator

At the beginning of this chapter I said that I had been entranced by the description of a bishop as the enslaved liberator of the rainbow church. At the end of a fairly detailed historical survey it becomes a more sustainable description of just what it can feel like to be a bishop in any age. Almost all have been appointed because they had something to contribute either to the church or to the society of their day. As leaders of churches with thousands of adherents, they had the potential to influence their societies in significant ways. Many were reformers or missionaries; even more were courtiers or had access to the courts of their monarch. By definition they had authority and patronage within their own church. Yet they also worked with considerable constraints. Whether it was the fear of losing the pleasure of their monarch or of the Pope, many have had to stand where compromise and accommodation to immediate need were necessary.

Modern bishops can identify with these situations and also with the aspiration which any leader will have. The feeling of being an 'enslaved liberator' is the lot of the leader. In our churches leaders are expected to defend tradition, give an example in holiness and also to be leaders in development and innovation. They are indeed enslaved by their position with its tradition and the constraints of office. They are also liberators inasmuch as they can use the influence, patronage and the legalities of their position to enable change and to end restrictive practices and the power groupings of cabals. They can create situations and appoint to strategic positions where change can be allowed to happen.

In our times, perhaps like the days after the Reformation, they are also enablers and leaders of a 'rainbow church'. Most significantly, senior church people have to be leaders of rainbow coalitions. The church is now made up of many nations and races. In individual countries, particularly in the western world, congregations are made up of an enormous mixture of people, all with their own access to information and to sources for spirituality. In the divisions and controversies which 'enslave' the modern church, no progress at all is possible without coalitions of differing groups. Perhaps the greatest challenge, and probably achievement, for the modern leader is to be able to go beyond holding together differing groups in their church and to bring about various levels of transformation. This can only be done if there is the greatest possible amount of openness and integrity in the actions of these leaders who are still significant public figures. The greatest danger which comes to us from history is for bishops to be seen as arising only from a small group in society, as being partisan or as being part of a self–perpetuating group or élite.

Modern models of episcopal leadership

The many images and pictures which episcopal leadership conjures up in the mind have to be defined, classified and grouped into meaningful and manageable 'families'. They have to connect with traditional models and expectations while at the same time be seen to emerge with at the very least a semblance of modern-day professionalism in the ways in which they are trained, developed and selected. In doing this, some clarity emerges about definitions of leadership in

a number of powerful and emotive titles. Leadership itself is essential
to any organization and has particular characteristics in large and
disbursed organizations such as churches. The most effective way
for leadership to flourish in such organizations is to link it with the
emerging idea of oversight, with its origins in the need for understood methods of responsible governance. Oversight is experienced
by those who form the leadership team and by all those who are
recipients. A creative way of describing this reception is to identify
models within different families of ideas. In this way imagination is
captured and energized dialogue becomes possible.

The interpretations or models of leader and of the ways in which
congregations will respond to leadership can be expressed in models
which both the leader and the follower can describe. In some of
the chapters which follow I want to set out the range of families of
'models', or concepts of leadership and oversight, which characterize
activity in an episcopal church. All of these will have a person who
is bishop as the representative leadership figure. Each will also have
new ways of looking at episcopacy as a shared responsibility. In this
way I want to point to a new way of governance for the churches
which combines my key concepts of leadership and oversight.

Many of the churches which trace their origins from the sixteenth
century Reformation, and some before, rejected the concept of bishop
and opted for a much more equal and participative form of leadership.
They wanted to do away with grand titles and the privileged lifestyle
which often went with high office. Through many debates there appears
to be a mixture of reasons for a denomination and its members to object
to bishops. Some of these are deeply theological and connect with the
equality of membership which is reflected in at least the spirit of many
communities in the early church. Others have objections which are not
about theology or about church order but which stem from the possibility contained in the temptations and corruptions of long-term or
absolute power. To this day the Methodist Church continues to debate
whether or not to have bishops. Internationally, Methodism is a denomination which has bishops, but in Britain it does not. The question of

bishops was significant in the Anglican-Methodist unity debates of the 1960s. The subject of oversight and governance was debated again by the Methodist Conference as recently as 2005.[15]

Whatever the age or time, episcopal leadership appears to have generally defined areas of responsibility which do not differ significantly with personality or cultural expectation:

- to preach the word of God
- to preside at the sacraments
- to admit and ordain to ecclesiastical office
- to exercise discipline
- to have pastoral oversight in the area to which they are called
- to guard and represent the apostolicity and unity of the Church's teaching, worship and sacramental life
- to have responsibility for the leadership in the Church's mission
- to relate the Christian community in their area to the wider church
- to represent the universal church in their local community

Who gets to be a bishop?

Most probably this question gets to the heart of why bishops in each generation come under such scrutiny. They emerge or are chosen from a large number of those who are equal in calling, rank or status – the priests. That they are relatively small in number will inevitably arouse both envy and admiration from those who were once their peers. The means by which bishops are appointed by no means gains universal approval, whatever the method. Appointment methods have not kept pace with changes in other professions or in industry and commerce. This is so much the case that next there needs to be a whole chapter devoted to the ways in which modern bishops are appointed and the responsibilities which they have. This will help us see the urgent need for a greater understanding of what needs to be understood in the contemporary exercise of *episkope*. There have been many reforms and these need to continue. One of those most respected and used in deriving 'models' of church is Avery Dulles SJ. In his seminal book, *Models of the Church* produced first in 1974 he says:

> The Church is not conceived as a democratic or representative society, but as one in which the fullness of power is concentrated in the hands of a ruling class that perpetuates itself by co-option.[16]

Similarly, in a recent book review in the Church Times, Robin Greenwood describes bishops as 'an elite appointed by an elite'.[17]

In order to understand what episcopacy is today and how it might be renegotiated for a future confederation of episcopally organized churches, we must now turn to a detailed examination of how leadership is exercised and how present day leaders in episcopal churches are appointed. We must examine the extent to which the lessons from history have been learned. Equally significantly we must see the extent to which the needs of the modern-day church are taken into account when job descriptions are formulated and when the requirements for the practitioners of *episkope* are detailed.

Notes

1 Messer, Donald E, *Contemporary images of Christian Ministry*, Abingdon, Nashville, 1989, p. 135.

2 Bultmann, Rudolph, *Theology of the New Testament*, Vol II, Nashville, 1989, p. 135.

3 Bultmann, p. 107

4 Frederic Austin Ogg (ed.) *A Source Book of Mediaeval History: Documents Illustrative of European Life and Institutions from the German Invasions to the Renaissance*, New York, 1907 reprinted by Cooper Square Publishers (New York), 1972, pp. 91–6.

5 Dickens, A.G. *Reformation and Society in Sixteenth Century Europe*, Thames & Hudson, London, 1966, p. 36.

6 See Duffy, Eamon, *The Voices of Morebath*, Yale, 2001, for the best

description of the life of one medieval parish in Devon gained from the churchwarden's and the priests records kept in the chest of the village church.

7 Moltmann, Jürgen *The Church in the Power of the Spirit*, second edition 1992, p 305.

8 See Duffy, Eamon, *The shock of change; continuity and disconti- nuity in the Elizabethan Church of England*, in S. Platten (ed.) *Anglicanism and the Western Tradition*, Canterbury Press 2003, p. 43.

9 For a sensitive description of the place of Hooker in Anglican thought see: Cavanagh, Lorraine, *By One Spirit: Reconciliation and Renewal in Anglican life*. Peter Lang, 2009, p. 12 ff.

10 *Four speeches made by Sir Edward Deering in the High Court of Parliament, 1641*, p. 8.

11 For a study of Milton's views on bishops see: Hobson, Theo, *Milton's Vision: the birth of Christian liberty*, Continuum, 2008.

12 Haliburton, John, *The Authority of a Bishop*, SPCK, 1987.

13 See the Papal Encyclical of Pope Leo XIII, *Apostolica Curae*, 1896.

14 Ramsey, Michael, *The Gospel and the Catholic Church*, SPCK and The Epworth Press, 1968, p. 39

15 *The Nature of Oversight: Leadership, Management and Governance in the Methodist Church in Great Britain*. Minutes of Conference document, 2005.

16 Dulles, Avery, *Models of the Church*, p. 38.

17 Greenwood, Robin, *Church Times*, 2 November 2007.

IV

The route to senior leadership

Vocation and ambition

While bishops and archbishops are the senior leaders in episcopal churches, exercising a particular role in the unfolding of *episkope*, it is from the membership of their churches that they are drawn and within which new leaders are shaped and called. Ambition is and should be a difficult concept for clergy. From the Prophets to the sayings of Jesus, there is plenty in the Bible which warns of the corruptions of power and the ease with which church officials can distance themselves from the spirit of their calling.[1] Yet churches are organizations that demand inspirational leadership and need to have effective administrators at all levels.

There are large numbers of talented and creative people drawn to work in church life, most of whom will only want to work locally. Many see possibilities to influence the wider society by leading congregations which exist to serve communities of those around them. Others come with entrepreneurial skills to build and renew congregations and develop the buildings they occupy. Those concerned with bringing the best possible people into leadership in the churches now talk about the need to develop more transparent and credible ways in which possible senior leaders can be identified, tested and given broader experience, ready for work beyond the local. In addition to descriptions about how denominations make the selection of those who are appointed, it is important to look at how ministries of *episkope* or oversight are understood within these processes. The potential for the exercise of *episkope* is an important element in learning how to be a rural dean, archdeacon, cathedral dean or bishop. While there should not be an overt striving for promotion among the members of any calling, it is responsible and right that those in senior positions should look for those with the very best in intellect and talent and create ways in which they may become the leaders for the next generation. This in itself is an expression of oversight.

Times have now changed, as have assumptions and expectations about how appointments are made. It is more common to expect transparent appointment procedures and the opportunity for suitably qualified individuals to be able to put themselves forward or be nominated for a job. However, what is right for a secular society is not necessarily always right for the churches. The appointments systems of the major episcopally led churches require examination, so that the merits and defects of any one system can be recognized and set alongside those used by others. In this way the vacuum in thinking about the needs of the church and the types of leader it requires can be overcome.

Not only do Church leaders have responsibility for their own members, they also have an influential position in contemporary society. It is a place which is changing and demands repositioning so that Christian leaders and leaders of other world faiths can contribute to the wellbeing of society, and remain as its conscience in the most effective way.[2] The ability to influence national life and comment on current affairs arises in part from the history of the office of bishop and archbishop and also from the personal charisma and expertise which many church leaders bring to these positions. The next stage in this study is to examine the appointments systems of the historic denominations and those of the Church of England in particular.

Appointment processes

It is not always easy to discover precisely how names emerge and how the appointment processes work for senior appointments in the different denominations. Often the boundaries between necessary confidentiality and desired transparency are difficult to discern. Denominations have significantly different ways not only of appointing their leaders, but also of including some and excluding others as selection processes take their distinctive course. The differences reflect in quite appropriate and describable ways how history and beliefs shape the ways in which leaders are identified and then appointed. We do need to ask if and how any screening processes in the denominations filter and exclude potentially suitable leadership candidates. The examination of appointments systems in the Church of England – which serves as the main subject of this study – will be analyzed in depth, with the Methodist Church and Roman Catholic Churches used as parallel instances for exploration. There will also be a look at episcopal appointments in the United States and in the Church of Sweden to compare and contrast different experience from Churches where bishops are elected.

The Church of England

In such a relatively flat organization as the Church of England, there has to be considerable interest in the ways in which candidates for 'promotion' – still called 'preferment' – are selected. Many enormously talented men and women will remain in parochial or specialist ministries for all their working lives, without any kind of public recognition from their denomination. Many – most – will not want to be promoted at all and are doing the work which they have chosen and from which they gain sufficient fulfilment. Some will want to take on wider responsibilities and be more at ease with such work, while others have to be dragged most reluctantly to wider responsibility because their gifts have been recognized more by others than by themselves.

In 2010 there were 8,170 stipendiary clergy in the 44 dioceses of the Church of England including the Diocese of Europe. A total of 373 senior posts are available as diocesan or suffragan bishops, archdeacons, cathedral deans and residentiary canons. It is predicted that there will be 7920 stipendiary clergy in post in 2012.[3] The numbers of non-stipendiary ministers, self-supporting ministers and those in paid employment, including academics, are not known with any accuracy, but are estimated to exceed the number of stipendiaries. The Church of England's appointments systems are changing relatively rapidly. Changes needed have been outlined in a series of Church of England reports and reviews. A detailed description of the Church of England appointments system as it is understood at the moment is contained in Appendix I.

Three Church of England reports are significant in providing current information and for offering a partial critique of its senior appointment processes. In 2001 Baroness Perry of Southwark produced a report from the Working Party which she chaired called *Working with the Spirit: choosing diocesan bishops*.[4] In 2007 Sir Joseph Pilling produced a report from the Working Party which he chaired about the appointment of suffragan bishops, deans, archdeacons and residentiary canons called *Talent and Calling: A review of the law and practice regarding appointments to the offices of suffragan bishop, dean, archdeacon and cathedral canon*.[5] In a less publicly commissioned way, the Clergy Appointments Adviser, the Rev John Lee, produced an appendix to his 2006 report to the House of Bishops entitled *From Frustration to Fulfilment* where he, with the members of the Senior Clergy Group, looked at the situation facing clergy in the last ten years of their ministry with a particular focus on those who might have expected preferment but who appear increasingly unlikely to attain it.[6]

The report by Baroness Perry, *Working with the Spirit*, describes in detail the system in place for the selection and appointment of diocesan bishops in 2001. It is severely critical of the unnecessary secrecy which surrounds the whole process. The report reviews the ways in which names for consideration are placed on a confidential senior appointments list and raises disturbing questions about preference and exclusion when the diocesan bishop is the only person who can place or confirm names on this list. It observes in a significant and critical way that the vast majority of those who have become diocesan bishops are already suffragan bishops. The group notes that: 'In the five years 1996–2000, nominations to 19 (43 per cent) of the 44 diocesan sees were announced. Of the 19 men nominated, 17 (89 per cent) were already in episcopal orders. Of the two men who were not in episcopal orders already, one was an archdeacon and the other a parish priest … Of the other 25 diocesan bishops in office at the end of 2000, by contrast, only 14 (56 per cent) were already in episcopal orders when they first became a Church of England Diocesan'.[7] This represents a worrying trend towards the most senior internal appointments being made from those who are already in senior posts. Some of the report's recommendations suggesting a wider gathering of information about a candidate and an initial process of open advertising have been taken up.

The Perry Report argued for greater transparency in many parts of the process, greater diocesan involvement and for a review of the place of the Prime Minister and the Crown in the nomination process. It does not explore the key subject for this current study and does not describe any corporate understandings of leadership and oversight, demonstrated in at least an embryonic way, which any group of Church of England leadership candidates might need to have. Instead the report focuses on the process; the lack of information about a candidate obtained from a wide enough range of sources; the weight placed on the nomination to the preferment list by one person, the diocesan bishop, and the inevitable opportunity for preference or prejudice to be exercised without external objective measures. Since there are no stated guidelines or criteria for selection, theological preference, acquaintance and chance meeting are described as playing some part in the emergence of names. Open advertising now increases the number of names which can be considered. There is no built in control to determine which selection criteria have been used implicitly in the identification of names, and as a result it is inevitable that some equally good candidates who might well have been considered have simply not come to the attention of the selecting group, would not think of putting themselves forward or have been dismissed without any objective monitoring of the process.[8]

The Perry Report comments that the route to becoming a diocesan bishop should not necessarily be through the occupation of a suffragan see. As such it comes close to recognizing another dimension of oversight which a diocesan bishop needs to have. It also raises the significant question of the difference between two types of bishop exercising different roles:

> We do not believe that translation from a suffragan to a diocesan see is necessarily a natural progression. ... Just as there are excellent suffragan bishops who are not suitable for translation to diocesan sees, it is argued, so there are also men who would not be suited to the position of suffragan bishop but would be excellent diocesans. It is not difficult to think of men consecrated direct to diocesan sees who have made outstanding contributions as bishops, but who, if they had first been suffragans, would probably not have been regarded as successful and might thus never have become diocesans at all.[9]

For now our concern is about the appointment process. Differences in role and function of bishops must wait until later in our exploration. Improvements or changes have now been made by the Church of England in its appointment processes. As a result of the Perry Report, candidates can now be told that their name is on the preferment list and a process of short-listing and interviewing is beginning to be put in place.

The report by Sir Joseph Pilling on other senior appointments looked at the various ways in which all other dignitaries come into post. He enters the complicated world of the relationship between the Crown, the two Archbishops, the diocesan bishops and the General Synod in the way in which appointments are made. Most significantly he identifies the need for the creation of what he calls a 'talent pipeline' which would establish a way in which there could be 'a national discernment process to support bishops in their identification of individuals with leadership gifts and longer term potential, based on a common set of criteria which clearly identify the skills and aptitudes needed for senior leadership in the Church'. Here there is more than a suggestion that oversight is a function arising from basic concepts and learned skills which need to be understood, and that in this sphere the church itself has a responsibility of stewardship:

> Talent needs to be nurtured and developed, and individuals need to be placed in roles which allow their gifts to grow and flourish. … we believe that, in order to be a responsible steward, the Church should adopt a more structured approach in relation to people who are identified as possessing the talent necessary for service in senior roles, so that leadership for the Church of tomorrow is being identified and developed in the Church of today.[10]

Pilling also explores a common theme with John Lee in his *From Frustration to Fulfilment* report. Pilling calls this theme or concept 'disappointment'. While affirming the appropriate place for ambition, he condemns the unnecessary levels of secrecy around appointment processes and the effect on those who know they have been considered, and even interviewed, but not appointed. He then refers to work being done to create the Lee Report and expects that this issue will be addressed in a robust but constructive way.

John Lee and his Senior Clergy Group write in an informed way, with startling examples, about the frustration and lack of realistic feedback which most non-appointed clergy get. The group describes well a good context for personal development and the restraint of personal ambition:

> It is important at this early stage to comment briefly on the sort of fulfilment that Christians may legitimately hope for – and, therefore, the sort of ambition which they may feel. Certainly the search for power or status contradicts the teaching of Jesus about not lording it over others and His own sacrificial death. On the other hand He advises His disciples to use their talents creatively and to build one another up in Christian fellowship. Talents need to be developed and employed to the best possible advantage. If recognition and reward can support this process so much the better; for example if appointments or honours are awarded on the basis of merit, the faithful and effective servant may receive recognition and reward, though these cannot be assured. His or her responsibility is to pursue a vocation none the less.[11]

The group develops possible ways in which experience can be used, and vocation to priestly ministry within the life of the local church can be reclaimed. The report makes a series of recommendations to bishops and directors of training about how clergy can be affirmed in their ministries, developed and trained for new church situations and supported in a life of partial fulfilment when work they had been led to expect was not attained. It does not explore and affirm the leadership already being expressed nor does it hold out the possibility of greater affirmation through a broadened concept of leadership and oversight. Instead the authors concentrate, as they describe their aim at the outset, to accompany clergy in the final ten years of their ministry towards a greater sense of fulfilment:

> Nevertheless, in speaking of predicament, there is a danger that frustration is overstated at the expense of fulfilment (or, at least, contentment). Discharging the onerous responsibilities set out in the Ordinal, however impossible, can be rewarding in itself. The

extent to which a priest understands and is comfortable in the
role is different for different people. One will envisage their role
as that of a Shepherd, another as a Servant, another as a Teacher
and so on. The group writing this report has therefore been keen
to ensure that the Church is not overly concerned with a problem
but instead takes the opportunity to reflect creatively, and without
emphasizing preferment, on ordained ministry in later years.[12]

Significant in each of these three reports is that the central question
of our present study about the extension of *episkope* to include a wider
spectrum of leaders in the church is not explored. The Perry Report
describes an exclusive and over-secretive selection process and makes
robust suggestions for more openness. The Pilling Report refers to
other places and reports where some of the theology of episcopal
ministry is explored, but concentrates on the need to establish a
systematic pipeline whereby talented clergy can be developed in
preparation for senior leadership. He does not explore the nature and
content of that leadership or the reasons for the selection of some
and the exclusion of others. Baroness Perry has pointed out that in
recent years there has been a disturbing trend for diocesan bishops to
be appointed primarily from those who are already suffragan bishops,
themselves chosen by existing bishops. Such evidence describes what
was becoming almost a closed system. Sir Joseph Pilling makes the
obvious but not yet fully acknowledged reflection about a system
which has such an exclusive route to inclusion and which produces
significant frustration:

> The danger is that this will result not only in the presence on
> the List of some clergy who are, in reality, rather unlikely to gain
> senior appointment but also in the exclusion from consideration
> for senior appointments of clergy who are suitably qualified but
> whose talents have not been recognised.[13]

It is this 'filter' alongside broader understandings of leadership
and oversight which gives rise for concern. The establishment of

broader concepts of shared responsibility will lessen the 'race' to join a hierarchy, reduce the feeling of 'in group' and 'out group' which prevails in the Church of England and will point towards the essence of leadership which will liberate talent at many points in the life of a Church currently under siege and experiencing a corrosive atmosphere of low morale.[14]

Of the reformed episcopal churches internationally, the Church of England is the only significant one where candidates cannot be nominated for election. It is now important to compare this system with others and with episcopal churches where elections take place.

The Roman Catholic Church

While the Church of England's senior appointments systems are gradually becoming transparent and open to much more public scrutiny, the Roman Catholic Church still retains a much more centralized process. The procedures are set out in Canon Law, particularly in Canon 377. When a diocese becomes vacant the Papal Nuncio resident in a country takes overall control. In practice it is the Vicar General in a diocese who oversees the day-to-day running, administration and decision making. No decisions are allowed to be made on unbudgeted expenditure other than relatively small sums. In effect activity and new initiatives are frozen until a new bishop is appointed. Local consultations produce names which are recommended to those responsible in Rome for episcopal appointments. The appointment is made personally by the Pope. The detailed appointment process is described in Appendix II.

I am not aware of any public documents reviewing this process or of any international moves which are proposing any significant reform. Comments can be found in the writings of some Catholic theologians and a few bishops. In these one of our basic concerns, the way in which bishops work together in what is called collegiality, is mentioned with surprising frequency.

One of the most significant public critics of a highly centralized

method of appointment is Professor Hans Küng. It is his view that
the 'spirit' of the Second Vatican Council requires more participation
by clergy and lay people in the process. He has gone so far as to
propose that the diocese itself should be the appointing agent, in
consultation with other bishops and the Secretariat in Rome. The
Pope, in his view, would then ratify the decision. His strident views
are an attempt to obtain greater collegiality in decision making which
he believes was the intention of the Council and has since been
subject to a systematic process of erosion. His opinions emphasize
the impact the Council had on him. He has devoted the rest of his life
to continuing to hold the torch for the 'spirit' of a Council which he
considers was a great step forward in governance for an international
body such as the Roman Catholic Church.

> In all this, the collegiality of church government which the Council
> 'in theory' fought for, in other words the collegial responsibility
> of Pope and Bishops for the whole church, is criminally ignored
> and passed over. This shared responsibility, grounded in Bible and
> tradition, called for by the present situation and affirmed by the
> Council by 1808 votes to 336, may have been celebrated as a great
> victory for the Council, but the Curia goes on working after the
> Council as if collegiality had never been decided on.[15]

In a more measured but yet still significant way Cardinal Basil Hume,
as President of the Council of European Bishop's Conferences also
believed in the application of the collegiality which was the spirit of
Vatican II. In his opening address as President in 1979, he asked the
question, 'What do the Second Vatican Council statements on collegiality mean for an individual bishop?' He went as far as suggesting
a pan-European symposium with all the presidents of the bishop's
conferences meeting with the Pope 'as a member of the College of
bishops, without his contribution being invested with definitive papal
authority.' It is said that the suggestion was received with interest by
the Pope but was not taken up as it might set a precedent which he
would not be able to honour at other events.[16]

The Methodist Church in the United Kingdom

Although not an episcopally structured church in the United Kingdom, the Methodist Church has Chairmen of Districts who have some of the same responsibilities of oversight. There are bishops in the Methodist Church in some parts of the world where such appointments reflect local leadership requirements. A detailed description of the Methodist senior appointments system can be found in Appendix III.

It is interesting to observe that John Wesley translated the term *episkopos* as superintendent and gave this responsibility to a person with oversight of a local circuit of churches. The constitutions of the Methodist Church in Britain and Ireland make it clear that *episkope* or oversight resides with the national Methodist Conference and in the Circuits. There have been many debates about the possibility of Methodist bishops in the United Kingdom, not least in preparation for the Anglican-Methodist Unity Conversations prior to the debates in 1969. As recently as 2005 the Methodist Conference received a paper on 'The Nature of Oversight: Leadership, Management and Governance in the Methodist Church in Great Britain'.[17]

There is a very real debate about whether or not *episkope* is the same in practice as oversight. This refinement has had its appropriate place in ecumenical discussions. It figures in a significant way in the question about how Methodist Chairmen could become bishops. Dr Colin Podmore comments as an Anglican theologian and national church officer in ways which point to a difference in understanding, or at least in interpretation:

> The Church of England's understanding of a bishop is not just as a superintendent of the clergy, but nor is the bishop's ministry solely one of *episkope* or oversight even in the broadest sense of that term … they are important not just in functional terms for what they do (overseeing/uniting) but also for what they are as successors to the apostles and as a focus for unity.[18]

Podmore makes significant statements about the historic and doctrinal status of those who hold the office of the successor to St Peter and who can trace their orders in an unbroken chain from the early church. He fails to distinguish significantly the wider potential of what 'oversight' can and should mean in an organization where power and responsibility are distributed. This broader meaning and application is the argument of this study. *Episkope* is more than being a bishop, and oversight is more than superintending the church and its clergy. The ministry of *episkope* is a shared and corporate concept which is the responsibility of all those given authority in the church. The bishop is the chief representative of that function, but is not the person who exemplifies the whole of the role.

The Episcopal Church in the United States

In the Episcopal Church in the United States (ECUSA) bishops are elected at diocesan conventions. A diocesan search committee conducts a trawl through information about candidates who have been nominated or who have put themselves forward. The search committee will identify and then nominate four to six suitable candidates. These candidates will tour the vacant diocese holding hustings and addressing meetings. At the convention candidates may or may not address the gathering. Clergy and Laity vote separately and an absolute majority (sometimes a two-thirds majority) by each house on the same ballot is required. The election is then confirmed by an absolute majority of the standing committee of the other dioceses in ECUSA. Relevant to this study is the fact that the dioceses of ECUSA are extremely transparent in the ways in which they select their bishops. The whole process is open and the selection processes are designed to be available for scrutiny.

The Episcopal Church in the United States is a good example of significant difference in interpretation of the role and work of a bishop and in the ways in which they work together. Cultural and historical differences play a large part in this. Within the one family of episcopal churches, with their origins in the Church of England or another European Church born from the Reformation, there can be many ways in which authority is exercised and in which it is received. In ECUSA there is a significant difference from, say, the Church of England in relation to authority. The Presiding bishop of ECUSA is not a 'primate' in the way that most other provinces elevate their senior bishop. He or she is not the occupant of a primatial see and does not have the authority of an archbishop who is a 'metropolitan'. That means that this senior national bishop does not have jurisdiction or oversight over the other bishops of ECUSA. Equally, although there are groups of dioceses in ECUSA, these are not 'provinces' in the way that dioceses are grouped with an archbishop in other parts of the world. As a consequence of this independence, diocesan bishops do not owe canonical obedience to any other bishop or group. In the debates and divisions of recent years this difference mitigates against a sense of collegial obligation and structural mutual responsibility for one another.

The Lutheran (Episcopal) Church of Sweden

One other example of a church which conducts an election for its bishops is the Church of Sweden, and is of particular interest since the church became disestablished in what it calls 'the great divorce' in the year 2000.[19] Elections are held in the diocese concerned. The electorate consists of all the priests who are employed in the diocese (they are legally employed by the parish(es) in which they work), the members of the diocesan executive committee and of the diocesan chapter and a number of lay people equal to the number of eligible priests, appointed by the parishes.

Candidates can put themselves forward or be nominated. Since the Church of Sweden has women bishops, all candidates must declare themselves 'to be willing to serve in every task together with others ordained to the Church's ministry regardless of their sex'. Through this declaration a commitment to collegiality is achieved as a matter of principle. A first round of voting eliminates those who receive less than 5 per cent of the votes. The Church of Sweden Disciplinary Board investigates the qualifications of those who survive to the second round. An absolute majority is required and if this is not reached in the second round of voting a final election is held between the two candidates with the highest number of votes. The Governing Board of the Church of Sweden confirms the election of the winning candidate. The election of the Archbishop, who is also Bishop of Uppsala, is the same, except that in addition to the priests and lay electors of the Archdiocese, the electorate also includes the members of the diocesan chapters and diocesan executive committees, and the votes cast by the priests and lay electors in the archdiocese are divided by ten.[20]

There is an interesting difference in the Swedish system of clerical and episcopal appointments. Even though no longer a state church, political parties, particularly at local level, maintain a presence in ecclesiastical decision making. They choose to have elected representation on the Church Council. Clergy are employed by the Church Council and the bishop has little or no say in their appointment. This presents a different kind of challenge to the use of *episkope*. The 'oversight' of a bishop is very literally that.

The way in which leadership and oversight have been negotiated in this church between bishop, clergy and lay people requires at least a mention. Sweden has a particular history of democratic and participative government, where the right of the people to participate in local institutions through their elected representatives is given high value. In the Church of Sweden there has been a long debate about accountability that has resulted in what is called a 'double line of responsibility' or 'common line of responsibility'. In this agreement the place of the clergy and the members of the church council are regarded as equal. The minister now does not chair the church council, and agreements made there have to be made in accordance with what is called an 'instruction' agreed at the time of the bishop's visitation to a parish. The relationship between a bishop and the parish which can be regarded as oversight, and the exercise of *episkope*, is made through this process of visitation. It overcomes the lack of sanction which a bishop and diocese has because clergy are not employed by them, and establishes a formalized relationship whereby the bishop is personally involved in setting the direction for the work of the minister and a congregation in a parish.

Personal influence and subtle means, primarily through the remaining right of parochial visitation, gives the bishop entry into the life of the local church. It is not unknown that, since clergy are appointed to parishes through the involvement of local politicians, they will bring their political experience to bear when making themselves available for election as bishops.

The need for professional development

This series of descriptions of appointments systems in a number of denominations shows that there is a series of networks, relationships and systems which supply people for senior leadership in the churches. The question which is being explored throughout this chapter concerns the virtues and difficulties in any appointment system. Underneath such a question is another about how suitable candidates are nurtured and tested.

A recent English commentator on the life and work of the clergy is Anthony Russell. His *The Clerical Profession*, published in 1980, was influential if not seminal in forming opinions and approaches relating to how clergy are supported and enabled to move through the different stages of their ministry. He was particularly critical of the Church of England's appointments systems as he researched them in the 1970s:

A recent career pamphlet issued by the Church of England stated: 'Unlike most secular organizations, the Church has no defined pay or promotion structure.' ... the general lack of accountability is a feature of the clerical profession and a point of significant dissimilarity from other professions... In contemporary society, the clerical profession has found itself unable to embrace many of the changes which have altered other professions in recent years and remains, in many significant aspects, in the form which it assumed in the nineteenth century.[21]

Russell concludes his well-informed study with a series of questions about the future development of clergy, and asks whether the clergy should continue to be called a profession if they are not subject to mandatory in-service training and career development in the way that members of other professions have become. Importantly, he also reflects in several places in his study on the question of whether it is appropriate, for entirely other reasons, to call the clergy members of a profession. He argues that this both separates them from the people they are called to serve and subjects them to expectations about training and competence which belong to more highly specialized and trained people such as doctors and lawyers. What he does describe is an attitude and an approach which slows or prevents training and career support for clergy just at a time when many of their colleagues and contemporaries are re-shaping the support given in parallel occupations.

Russell was researching and writing in the 1970s. The report by Sir Joseph Pilling, published in 2007, appears to be asking the same questions and still suggesting that the first step towards a solution to them would be a professional structure to support all clergy, but one which will also recognize and develop those who might become the next generation of church leaders:

> There is as yet little attempt on the part of the official structures of the Church of England to offer structured support, training and development opportunities to those identified as having potential to serve the church as leaders at the highest level.[22]

Career or vocation?

At the heart of this exploration is the balance between the describable needs of a church and the ways in which it selects, appoints and develops its leadership. Always a career or vocational concern for those who might want to be considered for wider responsibility is the balance between contentment in their present role and an awareness that they might serve their church more appropriately in another place. Traditionally, across many professions, and not unknown even among politicians, there is a reluctance to admit ambition. Overly ambitious members of many professions can be regarded as less than true to their own calling which it is assumed began as a desire for service to humankind rather than as a route to senior responsibility or to self-fulfilment. Many a bishop and archbishop proclaims in a self-justifying way, 'but I am really still a parish priest at heart'. Most politicians and not only those used for parody will protest that they have no personal ambition, 'but if my friends were to encourage and persuade me ...'

Peter Rudge writes perceptively about the natural feelings of many clergy who want to expand their areas of responsibility and have their gifts used in the fullest way:

It is not unknown for some clergy to feel a sense of frustration in their ministry which they might explain in terms of the lack of opportunities open to them. ... What adds to their frustration may be the awareness that other clergy have the opportunities and obtain preferment. In vocational terms, those who feel frustrated may be filled with the high ideals of their calling and genuinely seek avenues for fuller service, but often such desires are frowned upon as seeking promotion, which ill becomes a clergyman, or as ambition, jealousy and envy, which are also inappropriate in the vocational sector.[23]

When the responsible development of talent – and we might also say the testing of vocation to senior office – is not realized and when particularly able people appear not to be selected, then an understandable frustration can result.

Behind the scenes in appointment systems

There are assumptions even behind the choice of the kind of people invited to conduct reviews of appointment processes. In an additional and interesting way these assumptions are demonstrated also in the range of occupations chosen for comparison with ecclesiastical appointments. Equally interesting are those professions and occupations not used for comparison. The Perry Report and the Pilling report looking at appointments in the Church of England take secular and business models as comparisons. There are a number of other people who in recent years have made critical and constructive comments about ecclesiastical appointment processes. One of the first people to study modern organisational methods across the Churches is Peter Rudge. He is an Australian ordained into the Episcopal Church in Australia. He sees the work of a bishop or an archbishop like that of a senior executive officer, balancing a number of roles and responsibilities at the same time. A significant British person who has been instrumental in analysing the work of senior executives and of senior military officers is John Adair. He sees a senior church leader as the person, not unlike a military leader, who should define strategy and enable its execution.[24] Robin Gill, a person who has contributed much to understandings of the place of religion and the churches in contemporary society, says that lay people are influenced by bishops more than they are by local clergy since they see bishops as socially significant agents of change.[25]

Of particular relevance to the formation of thought about *episkope* is Charles Handy, a British management writer and consultant. He identifies the cultures of organizations as the places where leadership is developed. In an accessible and intriguing analysis of the different methods of working in organizations, he uses a kind of religious language. He writes about churches and congregations whose needs he groups appropriately into 'families'. He calls these 'gods' using concepts from Greek mythology, identifying a clubbable family culture (Zeus), a culture concerned with status and role (Apollo), a task-focused culture (Athena) and an existential culture (Dionysius) as underlying explanations for how leaders are valued and are developed or emerge in different places. These are each, but especially cumulatively, expressions of *episkope*:

> Many a church congregation has, in the best Christian tradition, proclaimed its threefold task to be one of worship, ministry and prophecy. All three are necessary to provide proper witness to a Christian presence in that place. What the congregation often fails to realise is that each task implies a different (Greek) god. ... There are really three different organizations needed, all under one umbrella. It can be done. The gods can learn to live together, but it is often one god who triumphs over the rest, so that in the end only one task is properly done.[26]

He makes the point that whether it is schools, hospitals, prisons, armies or parliaments, each demands a different cultural blend and a particular type of leader at a particular stage in their development. It is the task of any appointments process or system to get the best possible person in the right place and at the right time. When a right understanding is reached and an appropriate appointment made, it is this person or leader who can mobilize energy from others. They will be the person who has grasped the key concept of oversight, who governs wisely and gives physical embodiment to the concept of *episkope*.

To appoint or to elect?

The question of whether election or nomination is the better process for the appointment of bishops remains open. In modern times, with the emergence of democratically elected governments, comes the expectation that many other organizations will choose their leaders and representatives in similar ways. The Episcopal Church in the United States has a very transparent election system but still with the diocesan Search Committee having the responsibility for ensuring a balance of candidates and checking their standing in the church. The Church of Sweden and the Methodist Church in Britain have similar processes. It is important to note that candidates in the Swedish process all have to agree with and assent to the inclusive policies of their church. There have to be checks in any country which will prevent 'party' nominations dominating. Open election processes need to have checks and balances to avoid the polarization of dioceses with bishops always being of one persuasion. Their great virtue is that a wide number of members of the denomination and all the eligible clergy have a vote and a public stake in the appointment process.

The processes by which appointments are made divide into those where there is an element of public involvement by the candidate, leading to a voting process, and the systems where names emerge from a number of sources and go into private and confidential selection mechanisms. It is likely that different types of candidate will flourish in the contrasting systems. Those confident in their public ministries, relatively popular and with good communication skills will find it easiest to engage with hustings and elections. The processes of nomination may well have the advantage of bringing into consideration those who would not want to put themselves forward and this among other reasons might make them very suitable candidates. Added to all this is the assumption and expectation that there is divine guidance influencing and even in control of each of the processes. Further analysis and the testing out of appropriate concepts of the needs and exercise of *episkope* may well lead to conclusions about which way will be best in the future for episcopally governed churches.

The Church of England's system and the Roman Catholic system are ones where consultation allows a number of names to emerge. The difference is that the name or person under consideration has no part in the process. In fact in most cases they will still not know that they are a candidate for the appointment until they are offered the job! In the Church of England suffragan bishops may well be appointed through an interview process and could be part of a group of two or three candidates who are considered. The large difference between the Church of England's process and any of the others is the influence of diocesan bishops in appointing suffragan and other staff who make up the majority of those who move through the senior staff system.

Important in our review has been the airing of the advantages and disadvantages of appointments made internally and those made by election. It would be easy to say that election should be a preferred method for all senior appointments. There are strong arguments to support this; there would be a level playing field and all those wanting to move to another post could put their name forward or be nominated by others. Credibility would be very high if transparency were the main objective. However, we have also seen that there are many who would never put themselves forward for election to office. There are others with much needed skills who would never get more responsibility if they had to be elected. We have also seen that there is a danger of transferring the 'party' divisions of synodical government to the appointment of bishops. One of the virtues of an appoint-ments system with a national overview is that dioceses have bishops of differing theological persuasions to meet the needs of that diocese and of the wider church at a particular time. A system which allows all to apply – and to be given fair consideration – linked with an appoint-ments process which would allow others to put names forward to an appointments or patronage board would work well. There needs to be a form of national oversight of appointments so that a balance of type of senior leader is appointed across a province and that senior leaders are drawn from those working at many levels in their church. Eventually, a final process of election within a diocese will have to be developed. Diocesan bishops need to be provided with an able team of colleagues, appointed through a public and transparent process, ensuring that there is objective oversight in the diocese and beyond of those called to share in *episkope* with the appointed bishop. Such a system would ensure a range of types of ability in senior leaders and would avoid the continuation of the internal feeder mechanism which constitutes the appointment pipeline in many places at the moment.

The difference between all these processes and any secular ones is that all of those involved in any appointment will be waiting upon divine guidance for the right name to be chosen. Here a mixture of professionalism in developing leaders and transparency in creating as level a playing field as possible is intermingled with a prayerful process of discernment of the right person for a particular position. It is an acknowledged part of the process, testified to by the range of different kinds of people appointed, that leadership experience and proven talent are not always the measures by which some people are placed in responsible and senior episcopal positions in the churches. Time and experience can be the only measure of whether God's hand was in a particular appointment or whether a flawed system, by election or appointment, resulted in the wrong person finding themselves in a place that was particularly uncomfortable for them.

In a reflection of the consequence of a system of election in the Episcopal Church in the United States, former Archbishop George Carey, himself once a theological college principal, made an interesting reflection on appointment by election in his autobiography:

> The democratic process of appointment places a premium on success in building up impressive congregations, business management and preaching ability. Very few if any American Bishops come from academic institutions, either seminaries or university faculties. This is not a criticism of individual Bishops, but of the system. Although many of the Bishops were gifted and able people, very few had been formed by academic scholarship. The consequence is that when confronting intellectual and theological issues the American House of Bishops was inclined to deal with them pastorally and experientially.[27]

It is worth observing that in the United Kingdom in recent decades two of the leading Anglican theologians who became diocesan bishops, Stephen Sykes and Tom Wright, resigned and returned to academic work before they reached the age of retirement. Rowan Williams is an example of a bishop and archbishop who is a theologian. With some rigour he has encouraged bishops from a wide range of backgrounds to engage in theological debate. Leadership in theological thought comes in a necessary combination of oversight from academic theologians pursuing their own work and the leadership of a denomination influenced, to a greater or lesser extent, by theological thought and challenge.

How many bishops should a diocese have?

There is a modern English debate about how many bishops there should be in a diocese. This has come into more prominence in recent times through concern about the financial cost of bishop, usually borne by the national church. In most other places in the world one bishop for a diocese is the norm. More theological than pragmatic is the debate about whether or not there can be more than one bishop in a diocese. If a bishop's ministry arises from the priestly ministry of the laity and clergy in a locality, and if the title is always a geographical one, then the argument follows with a certain amount of logic that there should be one bishop for one diocese. This is the case in many parts of the world. In the dioceses of ECUSA and of the Church of Sweden there is a normal practice of there only being one bishop. Exceptions are made when the bishop of the diocese is also an Archbishop. The Roman Catholic Church follows the same principle with some exceptions.

In the Church of England, and to a lesser extent in the Roman Catholic Church, larger dioceses have been sub-divided to make Episcopal Areas where one diocesan bishop has two or three other Area Bishops working with them. There is a precedent in the early church where is seems that the bishops in Rome exercised a kind of

collegiality. Area systems are a kind of halfway house so that the Area
Bishop has real territorial pastoral responsibility. Tensions are inevitable about the actual role of the Area Bishop who is also a suffragan
to a diocesan bishop who, in spite of legal schemes where episcopal
powers are devolved, can seem to be able to cap or on occasions
override the decisions made by an Area Bishop.

The situation of suffragan bishops is even more open to critical
comment. Originally instituted in modern times to lighten the
workload of diocesan bishops, there is always an ambiguity about
this person's role. Many are appointed with a specialism to offer
to the diocese and to the wider church and have a freedom to use
their particular talent. Those appointed to lighten the load of the
diocesan to allow them to become more specialized or to exercise
a national role, have a more limited sphere of fulfilment, though
many are respected and loved by their people. There are occasions
when frustration can occur where a suffragan works harmoniously
with the diocesan bishop who appoints them but has less easy
relationships with the successor once the appointing bishop retires
or moves to another post. Many have also observed that a phase of
appointing relatively young suffragans resulted in many remaining
in the same post for up to 20 years without any prospect of a change
in work. Baroness Perry concluded rightly that the route to a
diocesan appointment should not necessarily be through first being
a suffragan. The unfortunate consequence of this for many suffragans
is that they are in post for a long time. A relatively new tendency is
emerging in a most healthy way where suffragans move to become
cathedral deans or to other national or international posts and gain
fulfilment and a renewed sense of vocation through the move.

A further complication in the appointment of suffragan bishops
has arisen through the fragmentation of church life over matters
of principle. Once women priests were ordained in England, a
system of appointing Provincial Episcopal Visitor (PEV) bishops was
conceived. This has resulted in a territorial system where more than
one bishop from the same denomination has pastoral responsibility.

The PEV bishops in England exercise their responsibility through powers devolved to them by a diocesan bishop and share in his overall ministry.

The point of view of English suffragan bishops is that their particular role in *episkope* is or should be shared in a collegial and collaborative way with the diocesan. Their own report produced in 2004 takes a significant step in supporting and developing the idea that oversight can and should be shared in a very visible way by all the bishops in a diocese. They see the task as a corporate one, with the diocesan bishop having the role of primacy within the group of bishops.[28]

Equally, with further divisions in the United States and other places over human sexuality and interpretations of scripture, whole dioceses as well as separate parishes have severed their ties with their denomination and formed new allegiances and new dioceses with their own bishops. Overlapping and sometimes non-territorial jurisdictions are moving from being the exception to becoming the norm. This is a new situation in the exercise of *episkope*. In one way it acknowledges the concept of 'oversight' in a modern world where networks and communities are recognized for other reasons than being territorial. It reflects an adaptation to the needs for oversight in dislocated communities. On the other hand this new phenomenon poses a complete challenge to traditional local geographical oversight of the people of God by one bishop.

There is an additional argument raised by Bishop Stephen Sykes and others over the jurisdiction of bishops. This is the ecumenical question, particularly when churches are seen as outward facing and relating to the wider community, that several church leaders – an Anglican bishop or two, a Roman Catholic bishop, a Methodist Chair, a Baptist Secretary and a whole range of Afro-Caribbean and Pentecostal Church Leaders, all exercise real *episkope* over a section of Christian people in the same area or region. Is there an argument here for the extension of a concept of episcopal leadership and oversight to be defined by a modern region and then exercised collegially and ecumenically? All this may seem like several steps too far. The only way forward is to determine what theological concepts underlie the principle of *episkope*, and then whether or not internal pastoral care of a subsection of Christian people overrides the demands of mission on a wider scale and a common leadership front in a region demonstrated by willing and principled corporate leadership.

Stephen Sykes states and challenges this situation with some stridency:

> Too much Anglican writing about bishops is about the episcopacy of a church which does not exist. If one takes merely the first sentence in the 1968 Lambeth Conference report on the nature of the episcopate one can see this problem. 'The bishop', it says, 'is called to lead the Church in the fulfilment of Christ's universal commission' (p.108). The question is, what bishop and what church? Can it really be said of the Anglican Communion that it 'possesses' the episcopate? In most parts of the world there is more than one bishop. If Anglicans are not saying that there is only one true bishop, and he the Anglican bishop, 'the bishop' who is the subject of this sentence and the whole section does not exist. … No Anglican should really be satisfied with any statement of the authority of oversight, which does not relate to the reality of a divided expression of church leadership.[29]

There is a tension in churches where there are archdeacons as well as suffragan bishops. The increased number of suffragans in some dioceses has called into question the distinctive and historic role of archdeacon in a diocese. Often in the absence of the sole bishop it was the archdeacon who gave pastoral care, inspected churches and ensured that the diocese was organized and run in an efficient way. Not all episcopally led churches have either suffragans or archdeacons. For example, in the Church of Sweden, without archdeacons, it is the dean of the cathedral who has a more prominent colleague role with the bishop. There visitations are done by diocesan staff and prepared by rural deans with the bishop conducting the final part of the visitation. As times become more pressurized with the diminution of the numbers of stipendiary clergy and the increased costs for maintaining staff of any kind, it is a proper and appropriate question as to whether the office and work of suffragan bishops and archdeacons might be combined into one appointment. Part of the increased work for bishops in the Church of England, and in some other provinces, is that the bishop conducts confirmations, the rite of entry of adults into the church. In the Roman Catholic Church it can be priests who act as episcopal vicars who carry out this function, and in the Church of Sweden it is the local priest who confirms. With the increasing advent of admission to communion of the baptized before confirmation, it may well be that this historic function associated with the work of a bishop has become redundant, however significant meeting a bishop may be in the lives of those making a new and deeper commitment of faith.

Virtues and drawbacks

Calling, ambition and means of selection are contentious areas for those who challenge accepted practices in church life. Nevertheless, it is right that there should be careful examination of training and appointment methods in order that the best people can be identified and appointed. The church is in very many ways a human organization and is subject to rivalry and intrigue in the same ways as any other group. The particular challenge, which should continue to be explored, has two imperatives. The first is that in an organization that has divine inspiration there continues to be the need for all the churches to listen to the changing spiritual needs of a nation or community, and to produce leaders who can teach, interpret and develop faith with contemporary relevance and a prophetic edge. That in itself is one form of *episkope*. The second is that the churches also have to be a model for the wider society. The way in which leaders are appointed and the ways in which they are held accountable for the trust placed in them has to be of the kind which other professions and occupations would want to learn from and introduce into their own systems.

There are episcopally structured churches and denominations all around the world. It has been appropriate look at some set in particular cultures and with recognizably similar understandings of *episkope*. The choice has been made in such a way that in parallel denominations different methods of selection and appointment can be described. Each of these has been reflected on in a number of ways and with reference to critical reviews which highlight some significant questions that can be described and evaluated. There is no doubt that each appointment method with its underlying assumptions about *episkope* has its history and background both in the culture of the denomination and in the country in which it is set. There are points for commendation, and reservations and criticisms of each. All add to our basic understanding of the requirements for the practical exercise of *episkope*. In this examination we have been able to describe the merits of each and also to outline the inherent dangers commentators and reviewers have discovered in each.

The mapping of a 'path to preferment' in any country has a number of identifiable and describable characteristics. This chapter has described some of them. The treading of this path is dependent upon:

- an understanding of the origins of leadership and oversight in the early church
- the theology of episcopacy which informs a church or Province
- the history of the relationship between church and state
- the assumptions about participative democracy prevalent in a country
- the strength and influence of the bishops as a group in a national church
- the level of outside influence which is acceptable from other Archbishops (Primates) or the Pope

- the level of state influence in selection of candidates
- the willingness of an individual to engage in self-promotion for an appointment, even if most is done on their behalf by colleagues
- the strength of opinion and lobbying from church political groups
- the cultural view of absolute power or collaborative/represent-ative roles embodied in the theology of a denomination.

In all of these descriptions we have examined the place of culture, history and denominational responsibility. If a danger has been identified, it is an over-emphasis on the individualism of a candidate. This can contrast with the requirement that appointed senior candidates have to act collegially. This touches on one of the original reasons for my embarking on this study: the questioning of understanding of collaborate working in hierarchical churches. Oversight of a national church requires that its senior leaders work collegially; the challenge for them as individuals and for the nature of the denomination which has appointed them is that they *believe* this is the most appropriate way to work. Whether candidates gain appointment by election or through a series of internal processes, the requirement of a collegial approach to their work remains the same. For this fundamental concept to be accepted there needs to be theology, experience and not a little pragmatism behind the refining of appointment processes.

Before and after appointments systems are called to account, the question about what bishops are continues to be asked. Essential for an informed and reasoned answer is as full a knowledge as possible about how *episkope* is understood and exercised by a denomination. These understandings influence the stated and the underlying assump-tions about suitable candidates for episcopal office. They might even influence the attractiveness of a calling to some considering a life of service in the church. In the next chapters we need to look at the understandings of *episkope* from other perspectives. It is time to explore the kinds of leadership and of oversight needed both by congregations and also by the communities in which churches and their leaders operate.

Notes

1 One such significant section is Matthew ch 23, vv. 13–36.
2 The power of church leaders cannot be compared directly with faith leaders in Islamic countries, and parallels with senior Imams are not always entirely helpful. The centrality of Sharia Law is more established and of a different nature than Church Law, which has always been separate from Civil Law.
3 Archbishops' Council, Statistics Department. Some residentiary canons also hold diocesan specialist posts.
4 *Working with the Spirit: choosing diocesan bishops*. A review of the Crown Appointments Commission and related matters. Church House Publishing, 2001.
5 *Talent and Calling: a review of the law and practice regarding the appointments to the offices of suffragan bishop, dean, archdeacon and residentiary canon*. The report of a working party chaired by Sir Joseph Pilling, Archbishops' Council, 2007.
6 *From Frustration to Fulfilment, the final 10 years of licensed ministry*, Senior Clergy Group, Chair John Lee. 2007. Archbishops' Council of the C of E. Although originally confidential, this report has been widely circulated.
7 Perry, p. 16.
8 The Rev Professor Canon Leslie Francis has carried out a number of studies on the balance of introvert and extravert personalities who become senior leaders. See *Personality and the Practice of Ministry*, Leslie J Francis and Mandy Robbins, Grove Books, Pastoral Series, p. 97. 2004.
9 *Working with the Spirit*, para. 2.8 p. 17.
10 *Talent and Calling*, p. 30.
11 *From Frustration to Fulfilment*, p. 13
12 Op.cit. pp. 19–20.

13 *Talent and Calling*, p. 24.

14 For a detailed description of 'in group' and out group' characteristics see: *Transforming Conflict*, Eolene Boyd-MacMillan and Sara Savage, FCL, 2008, pp. 23, 27.

15 Küng, Hans, *Disputed Truth*, p. 23.

16 Charles, William, *Basil Hume Ten Years On*, Continuum, 2009, p. 151.

17 *The Nature of Oversight: Leadership, Management and Governance in the Methodist Church in Great Britain* and *What is a District Chair?* Minutes of Conference, 2005.

18 Theology Journal, May/June 2006, Podmore, Colin, 'The Church of England's understanding of episcopacy', p. 173.

19 For a full description in English of the significance of the 2000 changes see: Theology, May/June 1999, Persennius, Dagmar, *The year 2000 Disestablishment in Sweden*, p. 177ff.

20 Prior to 1 January 2000, the Swedish Government chose between the three candidates who gained the most votes in the election. It was not uncommon for the candidate who came second or third to be appointed. (Source: *Working with the Spirit*, p. 158).

21 Russell, Anthony, *The Clerical Profession*, SPCK, 1980, p. 271.

22 *Talent and Calling*, p. 30.

23 Peter F. Rudge, *Management in the Church*, McGraw Hill, 1976. p. 30.

24 Adair, John, *Effective Strategic Leadership*, Pan, 2003. p. 35.

25 Gill, Robin, *Theology and Social Structure*, Mowbray, 1977. p. 100.

26 Handy, Charles, *The Gods of Management*, Arrow, 1995. p. 19.

27 Carey, George, *Know the Truth: a memoir*, Harper Perennial, 2005. p. 219.

28 *Suffragan Bishops*, Church House Publishing, GS Misc 733, 2004, p. 23.

29 Sykes, Stephen, *The Integrity of Anglicanism*, Mowbray, 1978. pp. 98–9.

V

The view from the pew

Essential to effective leadership – and oversight – is a vibrant reciprocal relationship between church members and their leaders. All too often relationships are described with a mixture of colleagueship, competitiveness, criticism and exasperation. The tension which exists between pedestrians, cyclists and motorists is quite similar. All are travelling along the same road, but how they describe the experience depends on who you ask and their perspective on the others. Parishes, deaneries and dioceses are all on the same journey but see each other in different ways depending on what they are doing. Parishes, or rather congregations, like a certain amount of autonomy for their domestic life yet come to value belonging to something bigger when they have a crisis of any kind or need external support. Deaneries have undergone a revival in recent years and have become a significant unit for planning of many kinds. They can often feel caught between parish needs and diocesan requests. Dioceses can be both hated and loved, depending on whether the discussion is about where the money goes or how a wider identity can be expressed. In all these the relationship is about mutual support and accountability. It is also about mission and relating to the wider world. In the introduction to a Curate's Handbook for an English diocese, one of the bishops has written, 'Collegiality is the foundation for fruitful ministry'.[1] Such a commitment could be a new way of describing the quest for collaborative concepts of ministry with which I began this book.

Such collegiality could be developed by gaining a greater understanding of the roles and facets of *episkope* which need to be present in the attainment of effective leadership and oversight. What these roles and facets of oversight are can be discovered by listening to the needs of clergy and congregations and through a patient trawl through the ways in which church leaders describe their work. I have called this section of my exploration 'the view from the pew', not because all the evidence described has come from congregations and their clergy but because without their consent no facet of the ministry of oversight can be fully effective.

The parish priest, the rural or area dean, the archdeacon and the bishop have a relationship with and a responsibility to one another for the oversight and development of their parishes. Equally important is the relationship of lay people to all these church officials, and many others, since they make up the vast majority of the membership, exercise most of the mission and provide a significant amount of the finance. In this development of an understanding of *episkope* the ways in which congregations expect and receive oversight can provide some basic models for understanding how this kind of church fits together.

The view from the pew to the pulpit, or the congregation to the altar, is not the same as the view from the pulpit or from the altar. That is because images of the leader are known in different ways by those who project them and those who receive them. In a similar way understandings of the types and characteristics of congregation or of church member can both help and distort the ways in which leaders will react to them.

Essential to the next stage of our exploration is the need to gain a view of how local congregations and their clergy relate to understandings of leadership in churches where deaneries, dioceses and bishops have the wider responsibilities of oversight. There are very many kinds of congregation and it is the history and story of many congregations in relation to their clergy which determine an approach to ecclesiastical authority. Anything imposed in most of these places is going to meet with some resistance. Local congregations and their clergy will question the actions of leaders who they recognize in a different way from that in which the leaders themselves may understand their authority and role. Tensions and misunderstandings arise from contrasting approaches to external and sometimes imposed authority. These tensions raise questions about which models of leadership or oversight can be legitimate and acceptable.[2]

In a conversation with Sara Savage of the Cambridge University Psychology and Religion Research Project (PRRG) about why different congregations and their ministers found it so difficult to relate to one another, a particular issue arose. We discussed how it could be that an organization, in this case a congregation, with the same professed aim of proclaiming God in Jesus Christ to a community town or city, became so unwilling to co-operate with other Christians. We asked, 'Why is it that a congregation of a different churchmanship or shade of theology would rather see the other go to the wall than offer resources or help?' Part of the answer can come from an analysis of different kinds of congregation, their attitude to one another and their approach to authority.

Different types of congregation have been analyzed and described by a number of research agencies. Perhaps the best known internationally is the Alban Institute in the United States.[3] In the United Kingdom, the Grubb Institute has a long and distinguished history of consultancy and research into congregations. This approach to authority has shown itself in many ways and is described well through a groundbreaking piece of analysis by Bruce Reed in *The Dynamics of Religion.*[4] Here he sees congregations oscillating between the need for dependence and the desire for independence. In episcopal churches, that tension and the debate which it generates is at the heart of a relationship between congregations and their bishops. It will take us to the root of the need or otherwise for *episkope* and will open doors for us to understand why parishes are as they are – part of episcopal churches, but different and often rivals in their work and in their expression of understandings of church.

We are given some new and general models of congregation in a book published by the Grubb Institute called *The Parish Church?*.[5] The authors suggest some fundamental differences in approach by parishes or congregations to authority or even to *episkope*. They call the different kinds of congregation Communal and Associational. In the former a bishop is seen as an integrating figure with a specific role between congregations who acknowledge a relationship with one another, and in the latter a bishop is regarded as some kind of administrative and liturgical official. This analysis has been one of the sources for me in the identification of difference in approach to authority and oversight 'viewed from the pew'. It has helped me in my attempts both to work out why congregations behave in certain ways and also to analyze how some church leaders can get it so wrong in attempting to relate to their members. Some of these fundamental differences in attitude go some way to explain sources of conflict internally in congregations and in relation to their bishops and archdeacons, and to other 'different' congregations within the same denomination.

Modelling effective *episkope*

Imaginative descriptions of differing types of congregation help us to see where our colleagues and those who differ from us draw their inspiration. We can use these descriptions to get inside the skin of those who differ from us. Equally it is possible, even if unwittingly, to create more distance through caricaturing another person or group, their attitudes, actions and imagined values. However, those exercising leadership and oversight in a parish or in a diocese can fall into the trap of self-fulfilment alone, and gravitate towards certain roles, concentrating on the parts of the job which interest them. The comprehensive exercise of oversight requires that a wide range of expectations are met and that a staff team is needed to carry them out. Patient and attentive listening and a developed understanding of the wide range of roles which need to be in play is required if episcopal churches are to feel that they are cared for, responsibly guided and led effectively.

It is certainly possible to get a person wrong, or even the culture of a diocese wrong, by trying to characterize them by imposing views or prejudices. These can give a distorted picture or a flawed one. If one exclusive model of leadership is imposed as an idea, it can be restricting and not allow for wider interpretations. To trap a leader in one received model can be enormously damaging to the possibilities for their work. Burdensome or restrictive models can even threaten the more comprehensive and varied understandings of leadership which any organization needs to have if it is to develop and change. There needs to be a health warning in any such analysis. The models described in this chapter are real in only one sense and that is to provide a 'mind map' through word pictures which enable data about the application and reception of leadership to be understood.

Grouping models into families can give a range and sophistication to interpretations of a type or style of leadership. They can add up to the kind of oversight which is needed, and together add to the comprehensiveness of care and leadership which an episcopal church – or indeed any church – requires. The importance of this exercise for the redefinition of leadership and oversight is that different styles can be assessed and sometimes chosen according to the particular challenges and opportunities which are being faced. At a more popular or understandable level, there are certainly those who react against the use of models, saying that they restrict the movement of the Spirit and that behaviour and characteristics can be transformed by God's movement in a place. They may well be equally right.

Oversight viewed from the pew

It is now possible to go on and describe the types and models of leadership which when well balanced combine to give comprehensive oversight in episcopal churches. I have chosen to try to do this from the perspective of the congregation or the objective commentator. In some instances I have included helpful analyses and reflections from church leaders with long experience of episcopal ministry. Other examples come from structured conversations which form part of further research I am conducting into understandings of *episkope*. All of this is underpinned in some places with appropriate biblical background material and references. It is by doing this, and through a historical and organizational investigation, that a route can be found to the underlying structures and mechanisms of episcopally led churches. By doing this it will be possible to explore the ways in which leaders need to be shaped and the training and support which they might need.

This is a kaleidoscope of models, some historic, others biblical and a few very modern that practitioners and recipients describe when leadership is exercised in the churches. They can be grouped into 'families' of understanding, leading to models of what is being described and experienced. Some models are little more than impressionistic while others are capable of intricate description and have been a part of the formation and structure of denominations and congregations for generations. All of the groupings exist and have life because they meet a variety of needs by congregation and sometimes community. They are places where individuals come together to articulate in some way their commitment to a religious belief. Using a very broad brush and with some licence, I describe and explore these in three family groupings: Organic, Directional and Authoritarian.

Models of *episkope* in leadership

Organic	Directional	Authoritarian
Gardener	Shepherd	Parent/Guardian
Chef	Navigator	Lawyer
Servant	Bridge Builder	Legitimator
Scapegoat	Missioner	Prime Minister
Speaker	Rogue	Monarch
Teacher	Interpreter	Prefect
Saint	Pioneer	

The organic family of models

The organic family of models encourages and gives leadership which is intended primarily to allow growth, both of ideas and in responsibility. It is a family which is characterized by ease with wide-ranging development. The organic family of models is one in which the leader and those who share in leadership and those who form the membership of an organization feel that they are a full part of it. Growth of ideas and of activities can come from many places. The phrase 'the encouragement of green shoots' might well be applied to the atmosphere, and there is a strong sense that something new will be produced which is more than the sum of the members. It will be a place where innovation and new ideas emerge, often through the cultivation of activity based on strong and deeply held values.

Gardener and Chef are inevitably words which will be identified with organizations and churches where a particular kind of growth and change are taking place. The leader who sets the tone of such an organization will lead by encouraging development and nurturing ideas.

The gardener spends much time preparing the soil in which healthy growth can take place. Churches where there is a high degree of personal interaction will be of this kind. Ideas will be welcomed;

not necessarily for their own sake but because they contribute to an atmosphere of innovation and experiment.

The leader, leadership team or ministry team will be representative of the strands of activity in a congregation where organic growth is taking place. The minister, who will be the acknowledged leader, but not in an authoritarian way, will receive ideas and allow them to be debated and tried out without feeling them a threat to their own position or authority. Such leaders will gain fulfilment through the acknowledgement that they have created an atmosphere where energizing activity can take place. In the gardening analogy, it is the members of the organization who provide the seeds of ideas, and the leader and leadership team who enable the right atmosphere for ideas to flourish. They also weed out the ideas that will not flourish and which could choke or stifle growth.

The chef produces and arranges the ingredients, the recipies for cooking and the resources which are the utensils for preparation. The leadership team might also negotiate, agree or bring from the good practice of another source, recipies which can be tried out. They will ensure that things neither overheat nor are too cool, and they will know and monitor the timescales for cooking. In such ways many different strands of ingredient combine in the right atmosphere, with the right objectives, for a manageable period of time, to produce something new, attractive and even appetizing.

The servant is a well-known and much discussed organic model for leadership. Servanthood is all about living as an example to show how others can be enabled to flourish through a leadership which is neither oppressive nor controlling but which draws its strength from exemplary living. Almost too much has been written about servant leadership. It is characterized primarily by the leaders showing high trust in their members and leading in ways which facilitate empowerment. The phrase 'servant leadership' was coined by Robert K. Greenleaf in 'The Servant as Leader', an essay first published in 1970. His work and ideas are now carried forward by the Robert K. Greenleaf Center for Servant Leadership.[6]

Its characteristics are demonstrated in the first essay which
Greenleaf wrote on the subject:

> The servant-leader *is* servant first ... It begins with the natural
> feeling that one wants to serve, to serve *first*. Then conscious
> choice brings one to aspire to lead. That person is sharply
> different from one who is *leader* first; perhaps because of the need
> to assuage an unusual power drive or to acquire material posses-
> sions ... The leader-first and the servant-first are two extreme
> types. Between them there are shadings and blends that are part
> of the infinite variety of human nature.
>
> The difference manifests itself in the care taken by the servant-
> first to make sure that other people's highest priority needs are
> being served. The best test, and difficult to administer, is: Do
> those served grow as persons? Do they, *while being served*, become
> healthier, wiser, freer, more autonomous, more likely themselves
> to become servants? *And*, what is the effect on the least privileged
> in society? Will they benefit or at least not be further deprived?

For the Christian the image and model of servant is most significantly seen in the life and example of Jesus. It is clear from his words
and in the way he set out his ministry that servant was a dominant
model. It is also clear from his words and actions and from the interpretation that his followers placed on his life that he quarried the
images from the Servant Songs in the book of the prophet Isaiah.

The word servant, *ebed* in Hebrew, occurs 800 times in the Old
Testament and means 'worker'. In biblical times servants were usually
slaves, the property of their master or king. In ancient Israel the
condition of a slave/servant was not demeaning. A slave might hold
positions of trust and responsibility as Eliezer did for Abraham. (Gen.
15.2) and, more well known, as Joseph did in Egypt. All subjects of a
king are his servants and we can easily see how this kind of biblical
language was used of everyone's relationship with God. Abraham
(Gen. 26.24) Moses (Exod. 14.31) and David (2 Sam. 3.18) are among
the most distinguished who are equally called 'servants' of God.

In the book of Isaiah there are four passages (42.1–4, 49.1–6, 50.4–9, 52.13–53.12) which take considerably further the concept of the 'servant of the Lord'. In these 'servant' poems the servant is the one who fulfils God's divine mission, which is not only to Israel but to the whole world. Here the servant, through suffering and death borne for the sins of others in a sacrificial way, then rises from death and is exalted by God. The consequence of this is that those who had rejected him see the error of their ways and recognize that it was this sacrifice which gave them their salvation.

St Paul makes much of this sacrificial servant theme in his teaching and guidance to the early church. He insists that the significance of Christ's death on the cross is that he paid a price and delivered freedom from slavery for all who believe in him (I Cor. 6.20, 7.23. Believers are no longer slaves but children of God (Gal. 4.7). This comes with a warning, especially for leaders, that they should not become slaves to others. (I Cor. 7.23).

The servant leader in diocese and denomination, parish and congregation will lead by example. Their values, and often the source of those values, will be experienced in a leadership style with the actions which flow from it encouraging imitation and a certain mixture of aspiration and admiration.

The scapegoat element in organic leadership will be aware of the dynamics of an organization or church, and of projections and false expectations. They will know that the great privileges which come with leadership are balanced with the isolation and blame, rightly or wrongly, which a leader and a leadership team have to carry. Without this essential element of the consequences of responsibility no organization can remain healthy and undertake organic growth.

Unwanted thoughts and feelings can be unconsciously *projected* on to another who becomes a scapegoat for one's own problems. This concept can be extended to projection by groups and certainly to the leaders of organizations and churches. In this case the chosen individual or group becomes the scapegoat for the group's problems.

In psychopathology, projection is an especially commonly used defence mechanism in people with certain personality disorders.

Interestingly, the scapegoat in biblical times was a goat that was driven off into the wilderness as part of the ceremonies of *Yom Kippur*, the Day of Atonement, in Judaism during the times of the Temple in Jerusalem. The rite is described in Lev. 16. Since this goat, carrying the sins of the people placed on it, is sent away to perish, the word 'scapegoat' has come to mean a person, often innocent, who is blamed and punished for the sins, crimes or sufferings of others, generally as a way of distracting attention from the real causes.

For the image of **Speaker** I am grateful to the former Bishop of Portsmouth, the Rt Rev Kenneth Stevenson. Reflecting on the work of a bishop, just before his retirement in the summer of 2009, he chose Speaker – as in Speaker of the English House of Commons, for one model which describes the work of a diocesan bishop.[7] It is the Speaker who oversees fair play and who enables a balanced debate to take place. This is an organic model of leadership in that there has to be someone who is in a position of authority, with the credibility and support of their peers, who can chair and enable a debate in such a way as to ensure that when decisions have to be made, both or many sides of an argument have been put. In a church where there are many differences and deep divisions about interpretations of the Bible, over the place of the ministry of women in the church, over sexuality and much more, there is an organic role for a leader to stand back from the heat of debate, preside over often heated discussion and who can make a way possible for progress to be made, often involving difficult decisions. The Speaker, while not giving any kind of a lead, can be as sure as is possible that winners and losers in a debate do not end with an overwhelming feeling that there is a victor and that the losers are defeated but that, through measured and well informed debate, a greater understanding has been reached, not only through the decision which has been made. The model is even more significant in the level of informed debate in the English House of Lords. Similar things can be said of Speakers in other parliaments in democratic countries. It is a model for parish or congregational debate and for denominational synod discussion of many kinds.

Teacher is a model where the enabling of the learner to learn and thus to grow is as significant in a particular way as the imparting of information from teacher to pupil. Indeed, learning and the kind of organic growth described here can only take place when both pupil and teacher are learning from one another in the interaction, and that 'knowledge' – which is very different from the accumulation of facts – is the outcome. Jesus' use of the Rabbinical teaching model rests strongly on the organic model. It consists of a method where question and answer are integral, and where the answer comes quite frequently in the form of a story or parable. The hearer or student is left with the responsibility for action or for a change of life. Frequently, Jesus' use of answer and of parable was not just to suggest ways forward or to help a person out of a particularly difficult situation; it was to reinterpret or go to the heart of what one of the original commandments God and of the community could mean for today.

Is the model of **saint** the only one which is completely identified by the definition and recognition of others? Clearly personal development and growth in spirituality form essential ingredients for sanctity. Sainthood or sanctity can have many manifestations and can be demonstrated in quite different kinds of life. What holds the definition and the concept together is that they are committed, through the deepening and outworking of values, to organic growth. They do this not only for themselves but they set up systems, in many instances, where followers can find models for their own development of values, spirituality and thus of growth. Not every saint would see themselves as a leader, though some most definitely did. Many saints are best described as 'thought leaders' who see things and the world, or even the church, in different ways. Through their ideas and by their example, leadership is given and organic change is effected.

The directional family of models

The directional family of models is precisely what it suggests. Here leadership guides and encourages people and enables them to move in a direction which takes them on to new places. The direction can be one which is a move on from seeming stagnation or confusion, or which finds new ways forward when nothing before could be dreamed of or agreed on. Directional leadership can also be visionary, and about hope for a better or different future.

The shepherd leader is following in a strong biblical tradition and is one where a clear mind picture can be conjured up. The image is not without its critics and, of course, belongs primarily to a past age. It can also be endowed with too much romanticism as a pastoral image from an age long gone. There are bishops who have said to me that they do not like to think of their people as sheep! The image does not demonstrate an appropriate modern relationship.

The world of the Bible is predominantly a rural one, so it comes as no surprise that sheep with their shepherds supply strong examples and imagery. There are almost 700 occasions when the words 'shepherd', 'flock' and 'sheep' are used in the books of the Bible. Only 100 of these are in the New Testament. King David began as a shepherd and endowed this image of leadership with special significance. The background for much of the imagery around shepherds as leaders comes from the context in which they worked. Sheep wandered because they were not kept in fields but searched for food, often in very sparse countryside. Shepherds were necessary to guide their flocks on to richer pastures. The scattered nature of the flocks meant that they were prey to wild animals and the shepherd had to anticipate danger or fight off the attacker. Parallels for leadership are clear. At night the sheep, sometimes two or three flocks together, would be herded into a sheep pen usually made up of loose stones built into low walls. There would be no gate or fence, and consequently the shepherd would sleep across the entrance himself. In the mornings the shepherds would call their own sheep and the large flock would divide. From this we get the origin of sayings about the sheep knowing and being known by their shepherd, of hearing and trusting his voice, and of Jesus being the gate of the sheepfold. (John ch. 10)

There are some key passages where this shepherd image is found: Eze, 34.1–6, Zech. 11.15–17, Jer. 31.10, 50.6 and Psalm 23. The task of the 'good' shepherd was to:

- have oversight of all the sheep
- strengthen the weak and protect the lambs
- care for the injured
- search for the lost and bring back those who were straying
- bring their sheep back into a united flock when they had become scattered
- lead them on to good pastures for grazing
- protect the flock from wild animals
- guard at times of rest
- regroup the flock for the next journey

In contrast there are passages in Jeremiah and in Ezekiel condemning shepherds when they fail. In Jeremiah these are at 10.21, 12.10, 13.20, 22.22, 23.1,2, 25.34–36, 49.19, 'Their shepherds have led them astray and caused them to roam' 50.6 and in Ezekiel at 34.2–16 'My flock lacks a shepherd and so has been plundered'.

In the Old Testament there are also references to God as shepherd. The most familiar of these is in Psalm 23: 'The Lord is my shepherd, He will make me lie down in green pastures'. Across many other books there are references to the sheep as Gods. In some places there are pointers to a future time when God will send another kind of shepherd, who will also be a king. Passages in Ezekiel 34.23 and Micah 5.5 are picked up in John 10 and a passage in Zechariah 13.7, 'Strike the shepherd and the sheep will be scattered' is used by Matthew in 26.31 and Mark at 14.27.

Jesus was himself aware of the shepherd-sheep analogy when describing himself and his ministry. Primarily in John 10 there is an outworking of the shepherd image as seen by him and a whole section of the early church. Here the good shepherd knows his sheep and the sheep recognize him as someone they can trust. The good shepherd is prepared to defend the sheep against attackers and will lay down his life for the sheep. In Hebrews 13.20, Jesus is described as the great shepherd of the sheep. Looking towards the second coming the First Letter of Peter (5.4) talks about the time when the chief shepherd will appear.

In the early church, those who became leaders were also described as shepherds. There are a number of references which are not just mentions but which come at pivotal and strategic points in the development of the church. In John 21.15–17 Jesus gives the charge to Peter: 'Take care of my sheep'. Paul's farewell talk to the Ephesian elders in Acts 20.28–29 commends them to 'Be shepherds of the church of God'.

Both Peter and Paul use the image of shepherd. Paul's teaching to the Christians in Ephesus was for some to act as pastors and stands alongside commendations for others to be apostle, prophet, evangelist and teacher. The first letter of Peter (2.25) gives theological weight to the image of sacrifice and of shepherding: 'By his wounds you have been healed. You were straying like sheep, but now you have turned towards the shepherd and guardian of your souls'.

The ministry of oversight of a group of people or a congregation comes as a strong concept in Peter's own teaching. In his same first letter (5.24) he says 'Be shepherds of God's flock ... serving as overseers'. This has immediate resonances when we look, as we have in other parts of this book, at ideas of *episkope* or oversight which are much more inclusive and could stand the weight of much collaborative reinterpretation.

The strength of the shepherd concept in leadership is that there are immediate connections for those who are in exposed positions of leadership today. The ideas universally linked with the responsibilities of any shepherd – of finding a way forward, of guidance and of protection – are there, as are the stressful experiences which come from takings calculated risks in order to guide and defend.[8] For the bishop, church leader or parish minister there can be no greater challenge.

For the model of **navigator** I am grateful to Robin Greenwood. In his book *Parish Priests, for the sake of the Kingdom*[9] he describes the parish priest as the kind of leader who takes and guides people on a journey, using navigational skills, but filled with confidence and hope about what for the navigator also might be an unknown destination. Greenwood selects the now familiar concept of *episkope* and takes it much further than an understanding of the ministry of bishops where he considers it has been constrained for too long. He develops the stimulating idea that the clergy and people in parishes or local congregations are the ones who exercise a kind of missionary oversight of the task of the church in the world. This is done by the renewal of local congregational life and a new understanding of the place and role of the priesthood within it. The base for such a rethinking is the local worshipping, eucharistic community.

Added to this re-imagining of *episkope* he explores 'models' which will engage with renewed concepts of priesthood, worship and mission. Greenwood develops the idea of the community with its leader or leaders as navigator. From his work in New Zealand and his reading of Anne Salmond's account of the eighteenth-century journeys of Captain Cook in the Pacific and of the eighteenth-century Pacific Islanders themselves, he came to see more clearly than ever that navigators were key to the expeditions. Those who navigated their way to and between the Polynesian Islands seemed to Greenwood to have something to say to us all. In a splendid phrase he says that they 'learned to navigate intuitively towards a destination, as yet unknown but attractive to them'.[10]

Bridge builder came to me in a renewed way in a note passed to me by Archbishop John Sentamu when I was addressing his staff and deans at Bishopthorpe Palace. In his definition from Luganda he included 'one who builds a bridge for others to cross the river'. I have later come to even more significant uses of the word, as used by the Mennonite Community in England who call their conflict resolution programmes 'Bridge Builders'.[11] The overall concept is a strong one and is about a particular kind of directional leadership. Here a 'bridge' can be built by the leader that they may not themselves choose to cross. They act as a bridge or they build a bridge which others can cross and move on to another place. The title 'pontifex' or bridge builder is one which bishops and archbishops sometimes apply to themselves. As a young theological student I first heard Cardinal Heenan use this mind picture in his enthronement address as Archbishop of Westminster.

The missioner is clearly a directional model. The clear intention is to move people to a new place. This differs from shepherd as a change in belief or world view is expected, sometimes in a dramatic way. This is in contrast to the organic pastoral shepherd model of leading to new pastures and refreshment. The missioner is a driven person or group, with a strong sense of purpose and a high sense of their values and beliefs. Missioners are needed in all organizations and in many parts of society. These are campaigning times and those with a strong vision for the future are needed to pioneer a product or an activity or to move an organization on when its main products are no longer meeting the needs of its market.

In religious terms, the missioner leader will share many of the same characteristics. They will have a strong sense of purpose. They will be driven by a high sense of the beliefs and values which speak to them. In the early church the missioner had a different gift or 'charism' than the bishop, priest or deacon whose ministry was more static and organic and sometimes authoritarian in relation to the local congregation of area. Missioner leaders want to see change, they are uneasy and restless with the seemingly static nature of many congregations, they will want to state and restate the values and beliefs which should be driving the Christian congregation and which should be drawing others into the community of believers.

The rogue leader is more than a catch-all for the non-conformist leader. This image was also first given to me by the Rt Rev Kenneth Stevenson. There is a need for 'characters' in the church as in most other organizations. The rogue leader may well be a strong individualist. This kind of person may well have been a leader in an 'on the edge' kind of congregation or group who finds themselves catapulted, often by force of their ideas or personality, into a senior position of responsibility. Rogue leaders are not comfortable with committees and often do not communicate well with their work group or team. Often – to the frustration of their colleagues, congregation or denomination – the media love them!

Rogue leaders have an uneasy relationship with their organization. They have a strong gift or talent which is needed and will bring innovation and spice to anything in which they are involved. They may have a low threshold of tolerance and will easily become bored. Rarely are rogue leaders team players.

Rogue groups exercising leadership may be a more modern and accommodated group. There is a more definite place in society and in the church for pressure groups or for groups motivated by one strong and reforming idea. Groups advocating ecological solutions to energy use or conservation have moved 'from the edge' much closer to the centre, as have groups advocating nuclear disarmament or a revised place for women in the ministry of the church.

Rogue leaders renew and refresh but they can be frustrating and controversial. Their low threshold of tolerance or interest in issues not central to them may mean that they are short-lived in senior positions or that they move on rapidly, or in a sadder way become sidelined when their innovative nature becomes distorted, or forced to retreat behind excessive eccentricity.

Pioneer has come more from conversations and interviews than any other source. It reflects perhaps the priorities and energy expenditure of the aware leader in any age. Today's leader expressing this concept to characterize their work talks about the need to push forward. They are aware that modifying and adapting old techniques and structures will not meet the needs of the present church or reshape a future one. They want to try out new patterns of ministry, to break time-honoured conventions and on occasions develop work which would not be traditional or easily understood in episcopal churches. Often the pioneer has come to want to be this model of leader through frustration at the gradual and organic ways of exercising oversight and leadership, and wants to begin to forge ahead and experiment with initiatives and with colleagues who want to see a church significantly different from the present one – and in a relatively short timescale!

Pioneer is a concept identified by reflecting on my questions about the use of *episkope* when I have developed my theme with some church leaders. They say that the opportunity to 'see over' (literally *epi-skopos* in our original definition) their region or diocese allows them to identify problems and issues more clearly. Often, while still working in a participative way, they can feel like pioneers because issues can appear clearer to them and they can see one or a range of ways forward.

The authoritarian family of models

The parent or guardian aspect of leadership is familiar to all. It is impossible to avoid receiving projections or expectation from those around. Some of these arouse dependency tendencies where the 'parent' leader is expected to fit both a family role and be an authority figure. Many feelings are aroused among congregations and team members that are not of the leader's making but that arouse feelings and memories from actual family experiences or from times when bullying or repressive actions have been experienced.

Parental aspects have many positive roles. They allow members to feel included and they can give an overwhelming feeling of security in which all can reciprocate and grow. We all need a variety of different relationships as we move through life and as we are enabled to work well in teams or to be members of vibrant congregations. Aspects of dependency and independency have been explored well and in a pioneering way by the Grubb Institute, primarily through the work and writings of its founding director Bruce Reed. His 'oscillation theory' already mentioned worked out in the seminal book *The Dynamics of Religion* has taken this thinking of the place of parent or guardian figure to interesting and challenging places.

Lawgiver is a convenient model for the legislative and disciplinary aspect of a leader's work. Organizations need to have a structure with boundaries. Around these are set employment legislation and many other constraints on abuses of human behaviour. The leader or leadership team has to reprimand and discipline as well as encourage. There is a special use of 'lawgiver' which, in addition to ensuring that there is conformity to regulation, requires that staff and employees conform to the mores and traditions of a church or organization. This is not to enforce conformity but to ensure standards and the distinctiveness which gives character and continuity are passed on.

Lawgiver is not an easy role for most leaders to embrace. It can be a lonely and difficult place. Decisions have to be made where all the facts cannot be revealed and where a sense of unfairness can sometimes ensue. One of the principal difficulties with the role of lawgiver is that the legalistically minded and those who like rigid structures can be all too easily attracted to the role, at different levels. 'Knowledge is power' and authority has to be worked with appropriate levels of disclosure. To keep information back for its own sake or to draw power around a leader is in the end unhealthy and counter-productive. It is a difficult balance to strike where collaborative working is aimed at and where the sharing of information is a part of the culture of an organization.

The leader or leadership team represent the values of an organization and are expected to keep to them in the example and tone they set for a church or any other company. Freedom to develop ideas can easily seem to be constrained by regulations and too familiar practices. The leader comfortable with their role and familiar with appropriate legislation can use laws and customs in ways such that change is enabled rather than prevented. Part of the genius of an inspired and inspiring leader is to create an atmosphere such that laws and regulations can be made to work for change, and when they do not, for them to be adapted or used in ways which do not feel like a straitjacket. Equally, the sensitive leader can prevent anarchy or direct disobedience by being seen to be fair and just in the application of laws and regulations.

Leaders legitimate change. It is particularly the role of senior church leaders, but also leaders in any place or role, to recognize change or new members or a change in the way things are done. Such legitimation is a part of the leader's public role and of their part and position in the processes of change. It is a key role in oversight which recognizes change and innovation and which blesses further development.

The leader is the person at the top and is thus **Prime Minister**. The comparison with the political leader of Great Britain and Northern Ireland is not completely frivolous. Like the Prime Minister, the leader, bishop and parish clergyperson is at the top of a particular tree. They are the public face of the organization which they are appointed to lead. In the end they are the ones who have to make some of the most difficult decisions. They have to speak in public about their organization and they have to represent it in the public square or arena. This role gives many privileges but also great responsibility. The privileges are more obvious than the hidden pressures of responsibility. Privileges include patronage, the right to appoint people to posts and to invite volunteers and representatives. It is a joy to be able to appear in public and to speak and visit on behalf of your church or organization. Doors open, and public life can provide opportunities greater than an individual might otherwise expect from their achievements alone. Responsibilities include having to take the blame when things go wrong, having to administer discipline, to preside over difficult meetings and, on occasions, to give public pastoral care in times of public grieving and bereavement.

Like the Prime Minister, all leaders have to work with colleagues. The group of Ministers with special portfolios or responsibilities form a Cabinet. All leaders need to select and appoint colleagues and with this needs to go significant and informed knowledge of their organization, its needs and how it works. There are crisis times when a leader is on their own and has to show how able they are to take responsibility and carry authority. There are many more times when a leader has to rely on and to trust their colleagues to carry out the duties with which they are entrusted.

Leaders on occasion have to be **monarchs**. Senior leaders are well aware of the public functionary role that they are called on to fulfil. There is no shame or embarrassment in wondering why a religious person sometimes has to play this role. Public life needs representative figures, and ones who have majority public acceptance and can be seen to be non-controversial and acceptable. Monarchs need exceptional amounts of humility to prevent them abusing their power or taking advantage of their role in inappropriate ways. It is a great privilege to be allowed by virtue of an office to represent other people. The humility comes in an appropriate acceptance of the role with due respect for its public place through heritage and civic duty, rather than from individual achievement or even of merit.

Prefects are people who do well at school and get rewarded. For my final model I am also grateful to the Rt Rev Kenneth Stevenson. The interpretation of his model, while taking further his original idea, is my own. Leaders emerge through their earlier and present work in an organization. Church leaders are those who have contributed to the life of their church in a distinctive way. Modern churches and denominations are run by committees and by synods in ways which could not have been imagined in any century before. Some present leaders, but many more from previous generations, have been appointed for their theological expertise, because they were good teachers, or even because they were trained as high-level administrators. Some saints have always got through the net. The churches of today have a tendency to be run by a preponderance of synodical players; hence Bishop Kenneth's model of prefect.

Here the principal issue is one of balance rather than of ability. The person who knows the system is a significant asset in any organization. To remain comfortably within a conservative organization makes or creates a certain kind of person. A church run predominantly by such people will be a cautious and conservative church, lacking in creativity and innovation.

The model of prefect is a good one, but it must be balanced with significant characters and teams of leaders who represent the other models. The test of any healthy and vibrant organization is to get the balance right.

From the bottom up

The many images and pictures which leadership conjures up in the mind have to be defined, classified and grouped into meaningful and manageable 'families'. In doing this some clarity emerges about definitions of leadership in a number of powerful and emotive titles. Leadership itself is essential to any organization and has particular characteristics in large and disbursed organizations such as churches. The most effective way for effective leadership to flourish is to link it with the emerging idea of oversight, with its origins in the need for understood methods of responsible governance. Oversight is experienced by those who form the leadership team and by all those who are recipients. A creative way of describing this reception is to identify models within different families of ideas. In this way imagination is captured, and energized dialogue becomes possible.

Each of the three families of models, Organic, Directional and Authoritarian, can be found in secular management thinking, even if some of them have different sources to support them. The difference in an episcopal church is that the structures of authority and the incentives to act are very different. There are different organizational characteristics, some of which are similar to commercial or voluntary activities but with some significant differences. Religion and layers of belief play strange tricks on relationships, some of which can hide themselves as matters of principle. What we have to dig down and explore is how it is that expanded ideas about oversight can actually bind a church together and enable creative interaction. Every description of a congregation, and every type of leader or model or symbol or image, points beyond itself to something else. We must now go on to explore what that 'something else' is in the many different places outside the churches in our communities where faith leadership and oversight are experienced.

Notes

1 *Curate's Handbook*, Diocese of Ripon and Leeds, 2010/11.
2 For a view of the types of modern congregation see: Cameron, Helen, *Resourcing Mission*, SCM, 2010. I have described these different types of congregation in much more detail in my books *Understanding Congregations* (Continuum), 1998 and *What they don't teach you at theological college* (Canterbury Press), 2003.
3 The Alban Institute is an ecumenical interfaith organization founded in 1974. It supports congregations through consulting services, research and publications: www.alban.org
4 Reed, Bruce, *The Dynamics of Religion*, DLT, 1978.
5 Grubb Institute, ed. Ecclestone, Giles, *The Parish Church?*, Mowbray, 1988.
6 Available from: The Greenleaf Center for Servant Leadership, 770 Pawtucket Drive, Westfield, IN 46074, Phone 317–669–8050, Fax: 317–669–8055, www.greenleaf.org.
7 Bishop Kenneth Stephenson expanded these models and ideas in an article for the *Church Times* of 4 September 2009, p. 11.
8 A full exploration of the use of the concept of shepherd as leader has been carried out by John Truscott. His article 'The leader as a shepherd' and other papers can be downloaded from his website at www.john-truscott.co.uk
9 *Parish Priests: For the sake of the Kingdom*, Greenwood, Robin, SPCK, 2009.
10 op. cit. p xii
11 London Mennonite Centre, 14 Shepherds Hill, Highgate, London N6 5AQ. Tel: 0845 4500 214, Fax: 020 8341 6807, lmc@menno.org.uk

VI

The view from the market place

As others see us

There is a certain fascination in seeing how church leaders are viewed by non-churchgoers. Many in public life find them an anomaly and, because they are unfamiliar with meeting clergy at all, experience a sense of awkwardness and try to distance themselves. Others treat them like equivalent senior leaders in other walks of life and respect them for their achievements. There are those who have an inquisitive sense of fascination and are genuinely interested because someone from a different kind of world has come into their experience.

It is equally important for a church leader to know what aspect of the activity of their church they are representing when they meet and work with business, government or community partners. In terms of being a leader they will have their own perceptions of the kind of thing a church is and how it functions. They will also be aware that many people who work with them from the wider community will try to categorize churches as organizations which correspond to something within their own experience. This is a deceptive and easy way to pigeonhole a church and even to try to imprison it in a caricature or stereotype. It is also an easy way to provide safety and to establish a comfortable distance. In the market place where the church is a partner organization among a number who are all working, or negotiating, for the common good it is important to know what can be offered from the Christian and faith communities, and what they need from community partners.

Ten years after his death, a memoir of Cardinal Basil Hume was published. In it he is said to have quarried the resources to keep him going through keeping a deliberate balance between what he called 'the desert and the market place'. His desert was not a wilderness where he wrestled with demons but the place of silence where he could meditate and deepen his prayer life. It was where his spirit was refreshed so that he could return to the other part of his calling as a church leader to address the challenges posed in the intricacies and compromises of everyday life. In this market place he knew that his resources would be tested to the full as he bargained, led, consoled and rejoiced with his people inside and outside the church. It was the balance of the two which made him the person he was, admired and respected beyond the Roman Catholic Church and far beyond the shores of Britain.

It is Hume's phrase 'the market place' which has given me the title for this chapter. Church leaders represent their denominations and dioceses in many spheres that are outside the confines of ordinary church life. Doors open for them to visit many interesting and challenging places and to join boards and committees as a represent-ative of the churches. These opportunities are not the icing on the cake, giving a refreshing escape from the hothouse of ecclesiastical life – though they may be welcomed in themselves as a God-given break from that – but an essential part of the comprehensive nature of ministry in churches which have a concern for the wider world as an essential part of the way in which they understand themselves. *Episkope* is an inclusive concept which embraces the oversight of the people of the church and also the people with which the church forms its communities. In such a way an enlarged understanding of *episkope* will include concepts of governance which involve a series of networked relationships with others who have the common good of the community as one of the essential ingredients of their work.

Exploring coherence

It is of particular interest to see how bishops who have just retired view their work. It seems to be the time when they are most able to take a balanced overview of the whole of their work. This slightly distanced opportunity includes a look at their ministries in the market place and in the church, and offers some clear views about what sustained them. One such writer is Michael Adie, who was Bishop of Guildford from 1983 to 1994. The book he wrote soon after his retirement gives a very strong pointer to the conclusion that the many different facets of his work come together to describe a ministry of oversight in the church and in the wider community. He says that his experience of a busy ministry left him with the uncomfortable feeling that all of life, and much of his work, was fragmented. He reacted strongly against this impression, feeling that it was contrary to God's purposes in creation. He also felt that his life as an exponent of *episkope* should have reflected integration rather than fragmentation. The title which he gives to his book is *Held Together: an exploration of coherence*. In it he wants to persuade others with similar responsibilities that their lives and their collaboration with the work of other people should be attempts to see where a God of wholeness can be seen and felt to be present.

> In any event, this experience of fragmentation and lack of cohesion in society and in the church must be confronted or we shall increasingly accept fragmentation as the norm. We must try to find a way through, a pattern of life which enables people to discover that integrity and cohesion which we so patently lack at the present time.[1]

There is immediacy in his words which border on the passionate. He laments the busyness which prevented him being more proactive during his varied ministries over 40 years as chaplain, parish priest, archdeacon and bishop. What he felt to be lacking is the very essence of our exploration. How is *episkope* to be exercised in the modern world? It is much more than the mere oversight of the people of God; it is certainly more than the preservation of an episcopal tradition by its present-day occupants – it is the development of a radical new concept by which many different disciplines and responsibilities can be held together, in co-operation with many partners; it is an exercise in creative cohesion.

Who is met in the market place?

There is not one market place but many. That is why we need many kinds of talented leader, each willing to trust one another as they represent the church in their own specialized but different market places. This exploration is more than finding out about where the resources can be brokered to enable churches to do some of their work. It is more than finding out with some accuracy about changes or crises in the world and having the ability to reflect in a theological way about them. It is certainly more than being confident of position and role in the church when leaders from other disciplines are encountered, and having the social ease to have a dialogue with them. It is about being a person in public life representing a church with the kind of long tradition of public service that can still open doors. Public arena is as appropriate a description as market place for where church leaders meet others and have something of their own to offer. Being a leader in this arena means encountering a whole range of other people who are talented and accomplished leaders in their particular sphere of activity, and being able to engage with them using a range of personality and academic skills which will have been recognized and sharpened as ecclesiastical responsibilities have grown.

In this market place or public arena are different types of people who have reached prominence because they have excelled in a particular activity and who have been given some kind of public recognition. In meeting and finding out both how to work with them and what they might want from the church, it may be helpful to distinguish leaders who have excelled in particular areas. Time Magazine, in common with a number of other national and international journals, makes an annual attempt at identifying 'top' people. In its edition of 11 May 2009, the magazine identified 100 what it called 'Leaders in a number of areas'. Their broad groupings give a convenient set of headings to catalogue the different types of people in public life that church leaders will encounter:

- leaders and revolutionaries
- builders and titans
- artists and entertainers
- heroes and icons
- scientists and thinkers

In other places in the same journal staff members questioned whether 100 was a sensible number to identify, or even if there were 100 such people who could easily be recognized on the international stage. These categories do ring true and can stand the weight of examination. It is probable that if 500 or 1,000 names were identified, the same categories might emerge. There were no church leaders named in the selection of 100. Church leaders might, however, be helped if these categories were expanded with recognizable if more general public life classifications to fit their own specialized and representational work. This will help to end the 'one size fits all' overconfidence of the church leader who thinks they can relate in similar ways to everyone. It will also help the church leader with sensitive and well-honed antennae to recognize different people in different situations and to begin to be able to respond appropriately.

Politicians – leaders and revolutionaries

Since the Christian faith has a concern for all aspects of life, leaders will need to be able to relate to the main public and political figures in their area of responsibility and beyond. Bishops, cathedral deans and archdeacons will be familiar with the weekly round of meeting local politicians, town and city mayors and other civic representatives. They will also have brokered alliances in their present and previous work with unusual and sometimes extraordinarily creative people. In doing this, and in building a critique of what they see, they will be doing no less than Jesus did in his earthly ministry. The difference from Our Lord is that they themselves have been given significant status by their faith community.

The pastoral support which church leaders can give to secular leaders is important and frequently gets high praise. Church leaders are in post for much longer than most other political public figures and have to keep a studied neutrality on party political issues. Their campaigning solidarity comes in working for a particular reform. This is not quite single issue politics but is similar. The principal difference when church figures are campaigning is that their work will often gain cross-party support.

The Jubilee 2000 campaign to abolish debt in some developing countries is a major example of church leaders forming an alliance with many leading politicians and radical thinkers. The success of this piece of strong lobbying rested on effective networking, a carefully orchestrated and well publicized campaign and a cause with which the public could identify. In their strident opposition to the Gulf War, however co-ordinated their voices, church leaders including the Pope had little immediate effect. In this instance it was important that church leaders were seen to give an alternative voice to many who were concerned about the legitimacy of this war and were not seen as naïve in their views.

Leaders in the professions – builders and titans

Time Magazine categorizes this kind of leader as one who will enter the fray and get their hands dirty – who will walk the walk and not just talk the talk. The enormous strength for church leaders as they join colleagues in the market place of public life is that they represent parishes, community and youth workers and interest groups based on the ground in their parishes. Many church leaders will have reached their senior positions because they have a distinguished record of such ground-breaking and innovative work in some of these places themselves. The advantage of the appointment of senior church leaders who remain in the same region is that they will already have relationships and have built alliances with others who have not gained distinction through their own career path. Less easy in the first instance is to arrive in a new region and meet people with great experience and strong networks in their locality. All who exercise positions of senior leadership rely on the support of their clergy and church members. This is gained, as is the essential information from the grass roots which gives credibility, by constant listening and regular local visiting.

The market place of national political and public life will bring church leaders into contact with many experts in fields almost completely unknown to themselves. High achievers in medicine, finance or the arts will belong to largely unknown worlds. Here church leaders will need to listen to the advice and briefings of their staff who have knowledge in these fields. It will be common for one senior church leader to have some previous experience of a discipline, art or craft and who will be the spokesperson on behalf of other leaders in topical specialized issues.

Leaders in the arts – creative artists and entertainers

While enjoying a certain and often disconcerting celebrity, church leaders will find themselves in the company of, and sometimes on the stage or in the radio or television studio with skilled broadcasters and entertainers. This is a heady situation and one with as many temptations and dangers as opportunities and rewards. It is always a privilege to be consulted and given a place in public debates. Key to the effectiveness of a church leader in such situations is that they have something real and significantly different to offer from other social or political commentators. Meeting and getting to know creative and artistic contributors to the culture of a community or a nation is an essential part of the work of an 'outward facing' church and its leadership. Churches receive as well as give in these places.

As with high achievers in the professions and in political life, there will be much that can be received and reflected on about the churches by such people. Their lively minds, creative abilities and wide vision can set long-held faith views in a wider and more interesting, not to say challenging, context. Creative people can often take an idea, and sometimes a religious concept, and give it an extra dimension. Church leaders gain much through these encounters and interpretations. Verse, song and canvass express deep faith experiences which need to come into the experience and then the vocabulary of faith leaders.

What will they want from the Christian leader? It could just be a reassuring and loyal companion to give constancy or continuity of relationship. Equally, and in possibly the same situation, someone who can spark creativity through their own personality and articulate a quite different perspective informed by faith and tradition can be what is needed. The worlds of politics, entrepreneurial activity and entertainment are fragile places and spectacular ups and downs occur in the fortunes of the participants. Loyal and constant support, sometimes with the critique of faith on a particular issue by a wise and trusted faith leader, can make a world of difference.

It is an enormous privilege to be invited into such company, and the intimacy and welcome can never be presumed. Inevitably there is a health warning about such work and these stimulating contacts. This is a claustrophobic and self-congratulatory world where egos are big and need to be massaged by admirers and friends alike. Some of this glamour can rub off on the church leader and encourage a cult of personality which will be liked by many church members and the press. The purpose of entering into this world is not to join it and bring some of its atmosphere into church life – there has always been an element of theatricality in the liturgy and in revivalist congregations which requires challenging – but to be a bridge and to make connections in which creativity can flourish and enrich the lives and creative abilities of all.

An event which brings together much of what I have described is a much-publicized court case. This concerns ministry to the arts. Bishop John Robinson gave evidence in favour of the publication of the D. H. Lawrence novel, *Lady Chatterley's Lover* in 1960.[2] He defended the publisher's right to make the book available to the public. Here he was using his theology and his wider ministry in a strategic way.

Leaders for a day – heroes and icons

Celebrity is a difficult thing. Church leaders will be confronted with whirlwind phenomena as people are catapulted to fame or are lionized by the public through some heroic act or media event. Sometimes it is best just to stand to one side and let it all happen. It is easy for the church leader to get sucked into inappropriate media events or stunts. On other occasions it is right to be alongside a celebrity just because they have a faith background or have sympathy for a particular cause.

Most often a pastoral relationship can be established. Contacts with people thrust into the media spotlight will be to encounter many who are baffled by what is going on around them. They will need a friend who has nothing to gain by making contact. Such occasions frequently involve people who have become involved in some national or regional event or tragedy and who had no idea what celebrity status was all about. It an encouraging feature of modern life, as far as the churches are concerned, that when a major event to celebrate or a sad but public bereavement has occurred, that it will almost be assumed that a service or commemoration will take place in a cathedral or parish church. It is of the greatest importance that the church or cathedral involved does much more than act as host to such an event, and that the staff, dean, bishop or parish priest, make their best possible attempts to establish personal contacts with those involved which will go on much longer than the event which has caused a media event or the need for an expression of public feeling.

National tragedies and the repercussions of war are never easy for church leaders on the public stage. Some have to be there and should never avoid the invitation to stand alongside the grieving and, on occasion, to express public sentiment and feeling. It is one of the expectations and responsibilities of state religions, official or not, that their leaders will officiate at times of celebration or of mourning. Not to be there, at the regional or local level, is noticed and will receive negative comment. Words said in sermons or public statements on these occasions can give a depth of interpretation to what is happening and prevent unhealthy or inward looking emotions, or even feelings of revenge or inappropriate triumphalism, to dominate.

Leaders in research – scientists and thinkers

In some ways it should be easier for church leaders to identify with creative thinkers and researchers. Many will have backgrounds in academic work at some early stage in their life and will have a familiarity with the world of ideas. Others will have made a distinctive contribution to one piece of work or another in an innovative way and will have made their own place in the development of a new idea. The initial or superficial difficulty of encounter to be overcome with some people in specialist areas of research is that they will never before have had close contact with religion and will associate it with repression and backward thinking. On the other hand, there will be some who are convinced of the Christian faith and who are church members, who are searching for some official support for their work and for an elementary understanding of some of the difficulties being faced.

There is a constant struggle, which echoes in tensions through the centuries, between new ideas and the received wisdom which a religion has blessed. There is, of course, the tension between biblical interpretation and scientific discovery and medical research, where churches have not always been clear in their support or forward-looking in their acceptance of new discoveries.

For the church leader there may be a tension between their sympathy with creative thinking and new ideas and the public stance of the church which they represent. Here personal relationships with scientists and thinkers are of the essence. The encouragement of research as an element in the continuing discovery of the wonders and possibilities of Creation is essential. Most frequent is the concern and debate about the application of new discoveries and the development of new ideas. There is no shame or disgrace in individual church leaders going out on a limb in support of a new idea or breakthrough.

There are many examples in our ecclesiastical history of church leaders making bold and innovative stands on cultural or political issues of international significance. There are now, as always, many areas of research where there are ethical consequences in the applications of scientific research. Faith leaders need to be well informed and to be able to give intelligent responses to scientific and commercial innovation.

Faith in the market place

Church leaders have to combat a general feeling that religion is in decline and has become so marginalized that its leaders should not have a stall in the market place. There has developed a view that the acids of modernity have eroded credibility in belief with the suggestion that faith in God belongs to an unsophisticated mindset. Knowledge of evolution and analysis of the biblical texts have eroded the platform on which credible belief can stand. The cruelty experienced in two World Wars and many others which are now widely reported, alongside the weight of human suffering which is both personal and universal, make belief in a caring, loving Creator God impossible. Church leaders and theologians have had to work in an atmosphere that, in the West at least, considered that secularization had triumphed over outdated and restrictive religious belief.

Secularization can be defined in a variety of ways. A strident and much quoted writer about secularization in the 1960s, Harvey Cox, then an assistant professor of Theology and Culture at the Andover Newton Theological School in Massachusetts, USA, gave this definition:

> It is the loosing of the world from religious and quasi-religious understandings of itself, the dispelling of all closed-world views, the breaking of all supernatural myths and sacred symbols ... the discovery by man that he has been left with the world on his hands, that he can no longer blame fortune or the Furies for what he does with it. Secularization is man turning his attention away from worlds beyond and toward this world and this time. It is what Dietrich Bonhoeffer in 1944 called 'man's coming of age'.[3]

When Professor Hans Küng began to map out what he wanted to say about this in the early 1970s, planning his *Introduction to Christianity* – which became *On being a Christian* – he said that we now need to move on to a new place in guiding the reality of a new situation where the analysis of Harvey Cox, which the two of them debated in Montreal ten years before, has been superseded:

> What needs to be given up, it seems to me, is technological progress as an ideology which, governed by interests, generates pseudo-rational illusions of what can be done. We need to give up science as a total explanation of reality ('world view') and

technocracy as a healing substitute religion. But what mustn't be given up is a concern for authentic human progress and the hope of a meta-technological society: a human way of working nearer to nature, a more balanced social structure and the satisfaction also of non-material needs, those human values which first make life worth living and cannot be quantified in money terms.[4]

One of the best known British examples of re-established faith leadership in this market place is between the Roman Catholic Archbishop of Liverpool, Derek Warlock (1920–1996) and the Anglican Bishop, David Sheppard (1929–2005). With the Methodist District Chair, John Newton, collaboration developed which addressed the social and economic problems of the city. Each came from a background of social engagement and had a wide hinterland of public influence and political contacts. Such was their influence that Prime Minister Margaret Thatcher and other senior politicians had to listen, and came to understand consulting with them to be important. Colleagues who worked with them replicated this example in other cities where they became political or church leaders. Their work is described in the jointly authored, *Better Together*.[5]

The market place of governance

I have come to the view that the best way in which church leaders can enter the market place and be effective is by understanding that they represent a significant network which is now understood as part of a worldwide community of faiths which have bargaining power. Modern Western society is made up of groups who need one another in order to achieve their aims and purposes. Without the inclusion of faith groups it is not possible to achieve some economic and many political results. Technically this is called Democratic Network Governance whose origins I have already described in Chapter I.[6] It is a relatively new branch of social science. It describes what many intuitive leaders and high-achieving groups have known for some time. It has direct relevance to the potential for effective leadership in the churches. Democratic Network Governance is based on the premise that progress is made in local communities and in regional and wider areas through negotiated interventions between a range of public, semi-public and private groups in society. When done effectively, and with some robust re-education, faith groups must be added to this list.

Most significantly for faith leaders, they find themselves at the point or place where the bargaining is done. It is church leaders, with openings to so many networks, who can be key players or agents in facilitating this. Faith leaders and church leaders especially may well be called upon with some regularity to offer pastoral support for those in trouble and to officiate on formal occasions, whether saying grace at dinners or officiating and preaching at great services; but it is their new opportunity as a broker and partner in the development of network governance where significant influence can be achieved. In our language and the language of this book we are describing an enormous expansion of the concept of *episkope* to move beyond internal oversight of a church to take a place in the arena of regional and national governance.

The great question for our development of leadership and oversight in relation to the market place is whether or not our church and faith leaders would want to own this significant role. A very important new opportunity is opening up here; it is now on offer for the churches to accept or decline. To participate in this way, however humbly or haltingly, is to attempt to give something to many people in the world who are bruised or torn by the fragmented nature of their work, and consequently of their lives. What those with ministries of oversight have to offer is an attempt at coherence. Their task is to reflect and sometimes to explain a God whose whole purpose is reconciliation and wholeness.

A church leader with experience and skill in resolving complex issues will be a natural contributor to governance networks. Church leaders can bring the essential knowledge and goodwill, particularly from grassroots networks, which is necessary to balance the political aspirations and wider unrelated concerns of some politicians. Church leaders will have particular skills in consensus building. Without these aspects of policy forming, governance cannot move on to implementation and seemingly firm agreements can stall.

Putting theory into practice

Such work is not of the essence of an internal church leader, concerned only with drawing people in and the nurture of members. It is of essential relevance to the leader who is part of a national or regional church where the care of all those in the community is a basic assumption and a part of the history and essence of a denomination.

The diagram below sets out the many networking relationships which a church leader needs to have.

The church leader and network governance

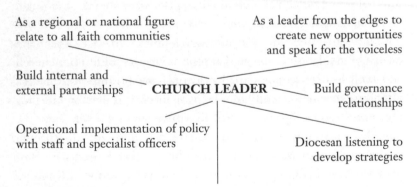

As a regional or national figure relate to all faith communities

As a leader from the edges to create new opportunities and speak for the voiceless

Build internal and external partnerships

CHURCH LEADER

Build governance relationships

Operational implementation of policy with staff and specialist officers

Diocesan listening to develop strategies

Staff development to create new network governance leaders

Some examples from recent history

A way of illustrating this more simply is to instance the ways in which some church leaders have contributed to effective democratic network governance in order to put some flesh on the theories. To do this I have chosen examples of the work of well-known church leaders from the recent history of our churches. None are still alive, though I may be inviting controversy through my choices and examples. I have looked for figures who have brought about change in this negotiated way and hope that they will inform present and new church leaders as they search for their own place in public life as a representative of their church or denomination. They are all people who have influenced and helped to shape my own ministry and thinking.

The market place of economics and national reconstruction

Archbishop William Temple (1881–1944)

There seems to be no disagreement at all that William Temple had the skill of chairing a meeting well, and an outstanding intellectual skill in being able to sum up at the end in a way that both expressed the consensus feeling, satisfied almost everyone and gave an extra energizing vision of what could be possible. Some of this skill was just raw talent linked to an unusually fine mind, but other parts of it sprang from an ability developed through a life immersed in the subjects he was summarizing. Temple was born to ecclesiastical privilege through his father, who was Bishop of Exeter and who became Bishop of London and later Archbishop of Canterbury. He also had entry into some parts of the English aristocracy through his mother, who was related to the Dukes of Devonshire. None of this was necessarily an advantage to his future career, as many sons and daughters have been overshadowed by high-achieving or well-connected parents.

Temple took this background and used it as a natural launch pad for the development of his interests and networks. He was familiar with many of the leaders of the day and was educated among the leaders of his own generation. At Rugby School he was a contemporary of the historian and economist R.H. Tawney, who became a lifelong friend. It was the University Settlement and social action movement, spearheaded by the Student Christian Movement, that inspired him as a young man. As Rector of St James', Piccadilly he was a contemporary of the creative and socially active Dick Shepherd, whose curates at St-Martin-in-the-Fields included the wartime 'padre', 'Woodbine Willy', Geoffrey Studdert-Kennedy and the future Bishop of Sheffield and SCM researcher, Leslie Hunter.

Temple developed political and reforming friendships and relationships with emerging thinkers of his day. He worked with William Beveridge on social welfare and housing reforms and with John Maynard Keynes and Stafford Cripps on economic issues. Temple himself, alongside his bible commentaries and writing on theology informed by Classical scholarship, wrote a number of books and pamphlets on economics. He was criticized by Prime Minister Stanley Baldwin when he and others tried to intervene in the miner's strike of 1926. His conferences, such as that for COPEC (Conference on Politics, Economics and Citizenship) at the Royal Albert Hall in 1924 and in other places, mobilized social thought and action across a nation. During the Second World War he produced an outline of how Britain might be reconstructed, long before there was any sign of victory.

His European networks were of an exceptional kind. He had been an active participant in the ecumenical movement through the 1920s and 30s. This gave him very strong contacts in Germany and Scandinavia as well as with the Protestant church leaders in the Low Countries and the Catholic leaders in occupied France. Temple died unexpectedly in 1944. Had this tragedy not happened, he would undoubtedly have been a leader in the civil as well as the ecclesiastical reconstruction of Europe.

This first example, particularly well known, of Archbishop William Temple gives one of the most public examples of network governance. He brought the ideas from an outstanding intellect and education to bear on the social and ecclesiastical issues of his day.

The success of his ideas, many of which were only put into practice after his death, bear tribute not only to his ability within networks but also to the permanence of ideas once established. The most robust networks can continue even when a key player is removed.

The market place of ecumenism and European politics

George Bell (1883–1958) and Dietrich Bonhoeffer (1904–44)[7]

Of the William Temple generation, and as significant players alongside him, these two church leaders demonstrate network governance in a particularly significant way. George Bell was chaplain to Archbishop Randall Davidson, and then a most creative Dean of Canterbury. There he opened the cathedral to the public on a regular basis for the first time on weekdays, commissioned artists and sculptors to develop work around the cathedral and invited T.S. Eliot to write a play about Thomas à Beckett which has become the international classic, *Murder in the Cathedral.* During his time at Canterbury and after, in a long episcopate as Bishop of Chichester, Bell fostered ecumenical relations across Europe and spoke up for the German people and against the indiscriminate bombing of their towns and cities once no strategic advantage could be gained.

Bell's international networking brought him into contact with the young German pastor Dietrich Bonhoeffer, who was to become a most influential theological teacher and writer. Bonhoeffer himself demonstrates network governance very well indeed. As a part of his own formation and development he held pastorates in Spain and in London as well as in New York. He continued this network, which was primarily concerned with international church relations, through the war years and, during his imprisonment, by letter. The plot to overthrow Adolph Hitler and earlier negotiations were developed through contact with Bishop George Bell and the intermediary and colleague networker, Archbishop Yngve Brilioth, in Uppsala in neutral Sweden.

The ways in which church leaders maintained strong colleague networks as they developed their early work meant that when leadership of any kind was needed on a specific issue, the contacts and methods of communication and decision making were already in place. At times of international crisis their colleagueship and moral stance was a public inspiration; even though they were criticized by others for strongly held views, they were able to speak for the oppressed and voiceless of their generation.

The market place of the industrial city

Bishop Leslie Hunter (1890–1983)

Also a part of that same ecumenical network, from his days as a curate at St Martin-in-the-Fields and as a SCM Secretary, Leslie Stannard Hunter was a very different kind of network governance practitioner. Shy and reserved by nature, he demonstrates that it is not only the extravert and natural public figure who can achieve national prominence.[8] As Archdeacon in Newcastle and as Bishop of Sheffield from 1939–62, Hunter used the ideas which he had seen colleagues develop in France about the mission to industrial workers through the *Mission de France* and the Worker Priest Movement to establish the Sheffield Industrial Mission. He was able to do this in his diocese because he had established good network relationships with the leading industrialists and trades unionists in South Yorkshire. He established a diocesan conference centre, Whirlow Grange, and a youth training centre, Hollowford in Derbyshire, through his knowledge of lay academies and laity centres in Germany and Holland. Hunter did the background preparation, created the contacts and then appointed talented people to establish the work in his diocese. Hunter is an outstanding example of one of the basic principles of leadership through network governance, 'to govern at a distance, through the mobilization, regulation and self-regulation of individuals'.[9] One of his key phrases was 'We cannot push people in front of us into the Kingdom; we can only walk with them'.[10]

The market place of network devolution

Bishop Gerald Ellison (1910–92)

The choice of Gerald Ellison, Bishop of London from 1973–81, may seem an unusual one. He was undoubtedly a person who could carry out the functions of monarchical episcopacy with ease, and was a public figure who commanded attention as Bishop of Chester and then of London. Many of his views about English society and the role of the Church of England in it were conservative. Yet he made several daring appointments of controversial figures to key parishes in London. In this regard Ellison is the kind of agent for change who sees clearly and acts decisively on important issues in ways which bring radical change. He was the creator of an outstanding devolved system of ecclesiastical administration in the creation of the Diocese of London's Episcopal Area System. London had for a century or more been regarded as ungovernable as a diocese. Its enormous size, six million people as a civil population, and the clergy which represented extremes in ecclesiastical party politics had led to many hiding under inefficiency and almost all doing exactly as they liked.

The creation of a system by which his oversight could be devolved to five episcopal areas was formative. In doing this he ensured that none of the authority of a diocesan bishop was undermined, but that some parts could be given to talented and trusted individual area bishops and archdeacons. The greatest network governance skill was to broker this, with synodical systems reflecting the needs of each episcopal area, and then to appoint able young clergy as Area Bishops who, with the experience of working in this way, all went on to run dioceses of their own.[11] With a completely different personality from the others instanced, but using the same governance tactics, Ellison was able to put in place the same method of devolution as Leslie Hunter.

The market place of the international city

Bishop Paul Moore (1919–2003)

Born with wealth and privilege in his family, Paul Moore had considerable potential to develop a career in finance or as an academic. Instead he used the social and cultural capital which was his by inheritance to be an effective leader in the Episcopal Church in the USA. From a tough parish ministry in New Jersey, with links and connections with talented 'social gospel' reforming clergy in Europe and the USA, he became a leading advocate for the renewal of the church in urban areas. His seminal book, *The Church Reclaims the City*,[12] sprung from networked experience of parish life and of his time as Dean of Indianapolis cathedral. It was published in 1965 when he had just been elected Assistant Bishop in the Diocese of Washington. By that time he was already showing an intuitive grasp of democratic network governance and was using phrases in this first book such as 'organized co-operation'[13] to describe work he was observing in urban initiatives across the United States. He had grasped network governance in an intuitive way before it had ever become a recognized theory and a social science. Moore moved to be Bishop of New York from 1972-89 and spent a campaigning life as an advocate for the poor and in pursuit of topical and radical causes. His use of organized co-operation developed, and he was instrumental in forming focused coalitions to fight homelessness and racial prejudice. He was the first to ordain a gay woman as priest and was a champion of inclusiveness in the church as a model for the wider society.

The significance of Paul Moore as an exemplar of the distributed and shared *episkope* is that he used his position and his networks as much or more in some of the key areas of political, financial and cultural life as he did within the church. His 'market place' ministry, occupying a major place as a public figure, demonstrates how much influence a bishop can have when well-informed and well-connected intrusions are made in pursuit of certain objectives. Moore was also a leader who did not use his inherited position, enhanced with individual talent and energy, to put himself at the centre of every cause. In deciding to bring about social change through a ministry in the church, he was immediately placing himself on the edge of where power and influence lie. It was through his secular colleagues as much as with his church associates that he achieved much of his reforming and campaigning successes. His personal life was not without controversy, and after his death revelations that he was bisexual caused a considerable stir.

Key 'ministry in the market place' characteristics

From the five examples above, and in the descriptions of network governance and leadership as oversight described before them, key principles emerge. They refine in an informed and illustrated way the place in society which any church leader can have. They demonstrate in a striking way the effective application of *episkope* through leadership and oversight, as expressed in the secular terms of governance, community partnership and the practical common sense of organized co-operation.

They can be described in this way:

- the desire to bring coherence to a fragmented world
- a wide hinterland of contacts often generated through friendships and alliances formed at an early career stage
- the development of social and cultural capital which give credibility
- the ability to bring ideas about changes which are well grounded in fact and which reflect change in other cultures and traditions
- strong partnership networks which are outside the churches they represent
- seeing their work in an international perspective
- working for the common good of the wider community
- bringing the resources of their tradition, faith and church to the network bargaining table

- the ability to create restructuring in such a way that the work is continued in an assured way after they have left
- not to work for personal benefit or to secure recognition or preferment
- a deliberate 'decentering' from most of the main activities which they have begun
- the deliberate development of those working with them so that they can take on more significant work.

This study would be inadequate if only the active parts of a church leader's work and ministry were to be described. It is of enormous significance that the areas of network governance which are described above gain a new credibility in an enlarged understanding of *episkope*. They will be sustained only if the systems of personal and corporate spiritual formation are also recognized and described. Ministries in the market place are not only the province of the socially confident or the politically motivated in the echelons of church life. They are of the essence of a credible Christian faith. This work is a natural development of *episkope* as network governance and as the oversight of all the work of God in industry, commerce, politics, science and the arts.

Notes

1 Michael Adie, *Held together: an exploration of coherence*, DLT, 1997, p. 11.
2 This episode is described fully, and with extracts from the correspondence of the day, by Eric James in *Bishop John A T Robinson: scholar, pastor, prophet*, Collins, 1987, pp. 85–101.
3 Cox, Harvey, *The Secular City*, Macmillan, New York 1966, p. 2.
4 Küng, Hans, *Disputed Truth*, Continuum, London, 2008, p. 204.
5 Sheppard, David and Warlock, Derek, *Better Together*, Hodder & Stoughton, 1988.
6 See *Theories of Democratic Network Governance*, (ed.) Eva Sørensen and Jacob Torfing, Palgrave Macmillan, 2008.

7 This co-operation is described well by many commentators, not least by Adrian Hastings in *A History of English Christianity 1920–1985*, Collins, Fount, 1986, Chapter 22, 'Helping German Christians', and in the chapters which follow.

8 See *Strategist for the Spirit*, ed. Gordon Hewitt, Beckett, 1985.

9 *Theories of Democratic Network Governance*, p. 39.

10 Hewitt, p. 140.

11 Each of Gerald Ellison's area bishops became diocesans: Mark Santer in Birmingham, Jim Thompson in Bath and Wells, Hewlett Thompson in Exeter and William Westwood in Peterborough. Many of Leslie Hunter's protégés, often called 'Leslie's boys' attained national fame: Alan Webster as Dean of St Paul's Cathedral in London, Stephen Burnett as national director of the General Synod Adult Education Board, Robin Woods as Bishop of Worcester and Dean of Windsor, Alan Ecclestone as a noted spiritual writer and 'communist' vicar, Ted Wickham as Bishop of Middleton, and Ronald Preston as Professor of Theology in Manchester.

12 Paul Moore, *The Church Reclaims the City*, SCM, 1965.

13 op.cit. p. 167.

VII

The view from the churches

One of the most remarkable things to emerge from my study of episcopacy is the discovery about how much recent work has been done on this subject by many of the denominations working together. As a result of their work it is possible to name and chart some new directions which are being followed. Our partner churches and denominations, episcopal and non-episcopal, have been doing their own work on the nature of *episkope* and the role of bishops. This needs to be taken into consideration and learned from as new directions are charted. We also need to look at what might be possible as the idea of an Anglican Covenant between partners in the Anglican episcopal 'family' or Communion is emerging. Each of these has the potential to provide a new commitment to leadership among differing partners through a renewed vision for the responsibilities of shared oversight.

Some substantial ecumenical agreements have been made in recent years. Relevant parts of these agreements focus on *episkope* as a shared leadership function and on the collegial nature of the office of bishop. There is one worrying feature about these positive and constructive agreements. It is that however much consensus those involved in the discussions have reached, and however much national churches and synods have accepted the agreements, it is taking some time for developed understandings of *episkope* to filter through into the practice of many in the constituent churches. Influential pieces of writing are appearing in some countries but these are becoming balanced more recently by conservative responses in other places.

There is a worry emerging that the substance of these ecumenical developments in understandings of *episkope* may have been put on the shelf by a new generation of episcopal leaders. As the changes and developments are discussed, it is this factor which emerges repeatedly when the theology and ecclesiology of different reports and writings are examined. There is a yawning gap between thinking and practice in the exercise of *episkope*. While the great thrust of contemporary theological thinking develops the concept that *episkope* is a shared work and that collegiality is a basic way for bishops to work, the practice of many who exercise *episkope* is doing more to develop a culture of self-management and individualistic leadership. Some reasons for this have been described or at least pointed towards in previous chapters while others have yet to be named and developed. This chapter will take us much farther into the territory of collegial, shared leadership and will then go on to identify some basic models for working which emerge very clearly from these ecumenical documents and agreements.

Baptism, Eucharist and Ministry

The last century has been one in which significant agreements have been made between the historic denominations as the movement towards greater mutual understanding has gained momentum. The beginning of this ecumenical movement is attributed to the Edinburgh Missionary Conference of 1910. Our starting place in this overview of agreements between the churches concerning *episkope* is with the work of the Faith and Order Commission of the World Council of Churches and its 'statement' or report on *Baptism, Eucharist and Ministry* (BEM). This was first discussed in a plenary commission meeting at Lima in Peru in 1982.[1] After acceptance it was published for further debate and agreement by member churches. It is significant that BEM did gain wide-ranging acceptance internationally in its three main areas of concern.

Important for us, and for any ecumenical debate, is that BEM makes important agreed points about the nature of *episkope*. At the same time there is recognition that much further work on the reception of this report needs to be done by the different denominations, since they have developed different interpretations and uses through the centuries. For churches in the Trinitarian 'family', the basis of all ministry is now agreed to be baptism. This is the rite which admits all Christian people and contains within it a call and response to engage with God and the Spirit in continuing the work of service and reconciliation revealed through the life and work of Jesus Christ. Denominations which have the Eucharist or Holy Communion as their central act of worship see the community of the faithful coming together for this sacrament as creating the place where all ministry is offered up to God and is transformed. Those who are ordained as deacons, priests or presbyters and as bishops have special and well-described roles within the eucharistic community and often in the society of faith within which it is set. These roles and responsibilities are described throughout as *episkope*.

Within the sections of the report entitled 'Ministry' there is an exploration of the calling of the Whole People of God and the role of *episkope* within the work of deacons and priests, called presbyters and bishops. This raises some key initial questions about how ministries of oversight are shared:

> The threefold pattern stands evidently in some need of reform. In some churches the collegial dimension of leadership in the eucharistic community has suffered diminution. In others the

function of deacons has been reduced to an assistant role in the celebration of the liturgy: they have ceased to fulfil any function with regard to the diaconal witness of the Church. In general, the relation of the presbyterate to the episcopal ministry has been discussed throughout the centuries, and the degree of the presbyter's participation in the episcopal ministry is still for many an unresolved question of far-reaching ecumenical importance.[2]

Here in this report it is significant and encouraging to see the concept of *episkope* come to the surface, and questions of relationship between the different authorized ministries raised.

One of the main strands of agreement within the BEM document and those which preceded it is that of *episkope*. The document states again understandings of the origin of *episkope* in the early Church and its communities. The description follows very closely our historic analysis of the origins of *episkope* in Chapter III and concludes that leadership in the churches was one of shared oversight. The bishop emerged in those first 50–100 years as the person who became, usually by election, the head of the local or regional college of presbyters. Throughout this document and in those which will be mentioned or described later, it is the shared nature of *episkope* which is stated and which still gives an underpinning and contemporary understanding to our theology. There is recognition that processes for the appointment of bishops from among the number of the presbyters has differed in the denominations according to their local and national history. Nevertheless, there is agreement that it is of the essence of the church that those appointed act in a collegial way to safeguard the doctrines and teachings of the Church.

There is stated in BEM a strong feeling that the existing threefold pattern of ministry requires continuing reform and revision in relation to its practice. Those who concluded this agreement felt that the collegial dimension of leadership within eucharistic and episcopal churches has suffered diminution. The authors make the point that the relationship between the presbyterate and the episcopate has been a long-debated subject throughout the centuries and is still for many an unresolved question. Their recommendation is for a further development of this collegial relationship – between bishops and bishops and between bishops and priests/presbyters, in order that there may be a more fully developed and effective witness of the Church in this world.[3]

In the instancing of the BEM agreement first in my exploration and description of new directions, I am emphasizing an important foundation. This is that the exercise of *episkope* in churches with a threefold structure is always corporate. With this position so clearly stated in ecumenical theological discussions and in BEM in particular, there are enormous difficulties when bishops take it upon themselves, or are appointed, to continue a particular ecclesiastical position within the church, representing one or another lobbying group. There are even more difficulties when it is the bishop of a diocese who chooses to lead their diocese into a schismatic position or into a place where they are no longer in a collegial relationship with their colleagues, their archbishops and with other dioceses and congregations. This is an international problem, experienced in its most acute form in the internal debates and divisions within the Anglican Communion. With bishops taking significant individual-istic stances, we may conclude that leadership and oversight will for the foreseeable future be exercised here within a divided church.

It is certainly the case, and probably always has been, that those exercising oversight will be doing so with those who disagree with them on some questions of faith and doctrine. The new situation in many places around the world is that these differences are becoming public, in a way that division is often a more attractive option than to work for unity and comprehensiveness. This situation arises even while in hard fought debate other agreements have been made which allow or even suggest the opportunity for a greater unity among episcopal churches. We now need to look at some of these other agreements to see the extent to which leadership and oversight are the characteristic interpretations of new directions in *episkope*.

The Porvoo Common Statement

In the most fortunate and helpful way for a greater contemporary understanding of *episkope* the Nordic and Baltic Lutheran Churches have been in discussion with the British and Irish Anglican Churches and have reached a common agreement about their episcopal heritage. The report for discussion and further consultation was published in 1992, and in Britain and Ireland is called The Porvoo Common Statement.[4] After thorough synodical discussion the report has been accepted by all the participating churches.

The focus of this report is on the work and ministry of bishops in their churches, with particular regard to continuity of episcopal ministry called 'apostolic succession'. It is important for many episcopally structured churches that they can trace the continuity of their ministry from the work and commission of the apostles themselves through to the present day. The descriptions of the apostolic roles in this report are helpful as we try to determine new directions for *episkope*. They are clear that one of the principal tasks of *episkope* is co-ordination. The many and increasing tasks which churches take upon themselves as they try to lead and serve their communities require holding together in some cohesive way. The agreement or Common Statement outlines how this responsibility can be exercised and how it relates in particular to the apostolic responsibilities and calling of the bishops:

> The ministry of oversight is exercised personally, collegially and communally. ... It is collegial, first because the bishop gathers together those who are ordained to share in the tasks of ministry and to represent the concerns of the community; secondly, because through the collegiality of bishops the Christian community in local areas is related to the wider church, and the universal Church to that community.[5]

In the Porvoo Agreement there is an acknowledged resonance and harmony with the text of *Baptism, Eucharist and Ministry*. The same set of phrases and theological concepts are used in the section on Ministry in paragraphs 26 and 29 of BEM where the *personal, collegial and communal* nature of episcopacy and the role of bishop are set out. These same phrases for the practice of oversight are used again in the 2001 Common Statement on Anglican-Methodist conversations.[6] In this way the first foundation stones have been laid not only for a development of *episkope* but also for a common basis of understanding and recognition between all Christian people. In our search for new understandings and uses of *episkope* these agreements give us this seminal set of three new and key concepts; that the exercise of *episkope* is personal, collegial and communal.

Episkope in the Roman Catholic Church

However significant new agreements about *episkope* are among the reformed churches that have retained bishops, the Roman Catholic Church is the place in Western Christendom where much of the classical teaching about episcopal leadership resides. It is a church with which less common ground has been established but where good and creative conversations continue to take place.

One of the best definitions or job descriptions for the work of a bishop comes from a document published in 1995. It also describes with some sympathy the problem – for bishops and their people – of understanding such a job and role in the modern world. The Catholic Bishops' Conference of England and Wales produced a significant report on collaborative working throughout the Church called *The Sign we Give*. It expresses a sympathetic understanding of the pressures and temptations which press upon the modern bishop:

> The role of bishops is not well understood in today's Church. People tend to see the bishop as all powerful and the arbiter of all decisions. This is reinforced by today's stereotypes of bishops. But this does not reflect the reality of today's Church, and nor does it fit with our theology. Most bishops work with a range of officers,

including lay people and religious as well as priests, whom they have authorized to take charge of particular activities, taking whatever decisions are necessary.[7]

The 'theology' referred to in the above passage comes from the Catechism of the Catholic Church, in the sections referring to the work of bishops. It stresses the collegial nature of their work saying that they are to be a focus for unity, exercising pastoral oversight of the people assigned to them, assisted by priests and deacons. Further, this Catechism which has authoritative status says that 'no bishop is an island' but each draws their authority more generally through being part of an episcopal college with other bishops who by working together emphasize the corporate nature of the Church.[8]

A long-running series of discussions between the Church of England and the Roman Catholic Church has taken place through what is called ARCIC (Anglican Roman Catholic International Commission). Much progress has been made in fundamental areas of doctrine and church practice. Here also some discussion has focused on episcopal ministry understood as historical succession in the selection and commissioning or ordaining of bishops by those who can trace their ordinations back to the first Apostles and St Peter himself. Apostolicity and succession has been debated by a working group of ARCIC and the results produced in the document *The Gift of Authority* published in 1988.

Ut Unum Sint – 'That they may they be one' – is an encyclical from Pope John Paul II which was published in 1995. Following the prayer of Jesus in the Gospel according to John (17.21–22), it dealt with the Roman Catholic Church's relations with the Orthodox Church and other Christian churches. The document reiterates that unity of the two historic churches of the East and West is essential, as is further dialogue which could lead to a certain amount of unity with the Protestant churches. This document confirms that the Roman Catholic Church is officially commited to unity in areas where common understandings can be reached.

In paragraph 54 there occurs a creative and visionary statement about the need to value contributions to church unity from the churches of the East and of the West. A delightful new phrase and picture was introduced which says that the Church 'must breathe with her two lungs'. In paragraph 79, subjects which are considered important for 'more clear' understanding that will bring unity, include sections on ordination and the place of bishops:

- *Ordination*, as a Sacrament, to the threefold ministry of the episcopate, presbyterate and diaconate.
- The *Magisterium* of the Church, entrusted to the Pope and the Bishops in communion with him, understood as a responsibility and an authority exercised in the name of Christ for teaching and safeguarding the faith.

The Church of England's response to *Ut Unum Sint* came in a booklet published in 1997 by its House of Bishops. In the commentary on episcopacy the response makes a positive and affirming recognition about what is regarded as the major landmark in the willingness of the Roman Catholic Church to establish ecumenical relationships:

> The historic episcopal succession is not an optional extra in the life of the Church. It is a sign of God's promise to be with his Church and a sign of the Church's intention to be faithful to the teaching and mission of the apostles (Section 43, p. 16).

In the guarded language of some ecumenical statements and responses there is here a commitment to continue special relations and dialogue with the Catholic and Orthodox churches which have an episcopal structure. The dialogue continues with the assumption that episcopacy is related to place and that the bishop's work and ministry arise from the geographical diocese of which they have charge and in which they exercise oversight.

It is intriguing to note a comment made by the Church of England House of Bishops in their response to *Ut Unum Sint*. At this early stage, in 1997 before some of the deeper divisions had emerged, they appear to be becoming aware that collegiality was under threat and that some bishops and archbishops were taking an independent position on some issues and consequently posing a threat to collegial solidarity:

> It is widely recognized within our Anglican Communion there is a danger that 'provincial autonomy' may be taken to mean 'independence'. Some consider that a primatial ministry with an appropriate collegial and conciliar structure is essential if this danger is to be avoided.[9]

What was then an interesting observation has taken a significant and challenging turn in subsequent events as deeper divisions within the Anglican Communion have emerged.

The proposal on Pastoral Ordinariates

New Popes can bring new elements and new challenges to ecumenical dialogue. Although Cardinal Ratzinger has been a significant person for many years in framing responses to possible changes in under-standings of church unity brought about through dialogue, it is only as Pope Benedict XVI that initiatives suggesting a different direction have been taken. One of these has provoked some controversy among Anglican Church leaders and those who thought they had reached a certain stage in Anglican-Roman Catholic dialogue on issues of joint understandings about key aspects of the Church's ministry.

This new initiative has been offered by Pope Benedict to the churches where internal division exists over the ordination of women to the priesthood and their consecration as bishops. In the Church of England, ever since the beginning of debates in its General Synod which looked likely to lead to the ordination of women to the priesthood, there have been organized opposition groups. Part of the legislation which was framed in 1992 was to give recognition to those who, in all conscience, could not agree with the decision. The principal lobbying group who had led the opposition was called

'Forward in Faith' and was made up primarily of members of the Anglo-Catholic or High Church group of the Church of England. An alliance was formed between this group and those evangelicals who, for biblical reasons about the headship of a Christian group, also could not accept women as priests.

Ever since the vote in 1992 there have been threats that clergy with their congregations would secede from the Church of England and look for alternative episcopal oversight. These have come from evangelical as well as catholic groups. In the autumn of 2009 the situation was offered a form of resolution when Pope Benedict XVI issued the document *Anglicanorum Coetibus*. In this he proposed the establishment of non-geographical oversight by Roman Catholic Bishops for ordained clergy and congregations who wanted to retain some of the ethos of being Anglican. Those congregations with their clergy who chose to respond to this offer would be cared for in new groupings called 'Pastoral Ordinariates'. There was little or no prior consultation about this offer and it was evident that ecumenical discussion between the Anglican and Roman Catholic Churches had not previously seen this as a timely and appropriate solution. This situation became very live when, in July 2010, the Church of England voted in favour of moving to the next stage enabling women to become bishops and proposed a more localized provision for alternative episcopal oversight.

What is important for our study is that with this offer we see a further development or adaptation of the concept of episcopacy. Here episcopal care could be provided for a group of clergy and congregations who were disaffected and separated from their parent body and its bishops, but who did not want to move to a complete and different form of membership and episcopal oversight in another denomination. *Episkope* in this application reflects or accepts a divided church and offers a possible new form of church order with a new form of episcopal oversight in non-geographical jurisdictions.

Time will tell if this is an appropriate or acceptable development, or if the offer contained in *Anglicanorum Coetibus* will be taken up on any large scale. Its very existence takes us another step forward in acknowledging that episcopacy and episcopal oversight is changing. It is just possible that, in a world with divisions which stem from deeply held values and where many congregate in groups around a single issue, this is a shape for the church which reflects a changed and changing role for *episkope*. Equally, these seemingly divisive situations may reflect a time of transition. There may have to be a large element of divinely guided 'messiness' before new structures for pastoral care, teaching, governance and leadership can emerge in a general and universally accepted way.

Episkope in non-episcopal churches

Non-episcopal churches have participated in ecumenical debates and produced their own statements about episcopacy. Currently the Moderator, Chairman or President in non-episcopally led churches do not hold their office for life in the same way as bishops do. The use of the words 'moderator', 'superintendent' and 'chairman' by many of the Free Churches is interesting and has strong resonances with role and office in the early church, many of which were revisited at the Reformation or after. John Calvin in Geneva established a new kind of civic and church government, with Elders and Deacons and a Council to govern the city. Churches called Presbyterian take their theology and church structure from Calvin and Geneva. The Scottish Presbyterian Church has lay elders and deacons. These make up a presbytery, then a Synod and a General Assembly. The Reformed Evangelical Churches in Northern Germany have a structure with bishops but not with an emphasis on historic succession in the way that most other episcopal churches have. Major agreements were made in what are called 'conversations' with the North German Protestant Church as a result of the work of the Meissen Commission which produced its substantial report in 1988.[10] The Reiully Common Statement of 1997 commits the

French Reformed and Lutheran Churches to further dialogue. While the exchange of pulpits and a welcome at the eucharistic table is accepted, the exchange or mutual recognition of ministries was seen as coming only at a further stage. The text of the agreement states, however, that 'all our churches are in change and are in the process of considering the balance between the various dimensions of oversight (*episkope*)'.

The Methodist Church and the Church of England have been engaged in active dialogue for more than 50 years. John Wesley gave his own translation and interpretation to *episkope*. He gave the word 'superintendent' to the minister with oversight of groups of local congregations, with their ministers taking literally the translation of *epi-skopos* – to 'see-over'. While remaining an Anglican throughout his life, he could see the need for local organization in the congregations he and Charles had created. Alongside an itinerant ministry, local churches had stewards for their governance. The groupings of congregations in 'Circuits' were organized and co-ordinated not by local bishops but by these Superintendents. In making this decision and translation, he was deciding on an informed return to a modelling of the structure of the early church.

In the Anglican-Methodist 'conversations' of the 1960s in England, Scotland and Wales the Methodist view of the present role and function of bishops in relation to the practice of the Church of England is helpful:

(123) All episcopacy belongs to Christ, the Good Shepherd, and the bishop's commission by Christ expressly assigns him to be the chief pastor of the ministers and people in his charge. As father-in-God to both he is called to feed the flock of Christ in tender concern for their well-being, not as lord and master, but as a servant of the servants of Christ.

(124) Both as pastor and guardian the bishop must, wherever necessary, within the framework of the Methodist Connexion, see that discipline is exercised within the fellowship of the Church,

and that in all such matters every proper step is taken to heal, forgive, restore, or, when all else fails, to rebuke, reprimand, or exclude. Discipline includes not only the proper operation of church courts, and the pastoral care of those who have erred, but the oversight of preaching and the supervision of public worship.

(125) Continuity with the historic episcopate will both initially and thereafter be effectively maintained, it being understood that no one particular interpretation of the historic episcopate as accepted by the Methodist Chuch is thereby implied, or shall be demanded from any minister or member of it.[11]

Anglican – Methodist Church debates about *episkope*

In the Anglican–Methodist discussions with reports in 1968 and 2001 there were Five Points about episcopacy from which Anglicans felt they could not depart and to which Methodists could accede:

- the episcopate symbolizes in an abiding form the apostolic mission and authority of the church
- to guard against erroneous teaching
- to be a symbol of unity representing the Church to his diocese and his diocese to the Church
- to represent the Good Shepherd as chief pastor in the diocese
- to ordain and ensure continuity of the apostolic mission of the Church

These debates were enormously fruitful and have led the Methodist Church to produce some of the most thoroughly researched documents and reports on episcopacy.[12] Anglican-Methodist dialogue continues, and has had the great advantage of bringing a focus to thinking on many key theological and ecclesiological subjects. In particular the work of clarification about the work and role of bishops has helped both churches to deepen and articulate their understandings. The situation between Anglicans and Methodists is one particular to Britain, and the history of separation and controversy over the place of bishops has had a necessary influence on the debates and the conclusions reached.

In other parts of the world, where history and tradition are different, there exist Methodist bishops who fulfil important roles in their churches and in public life. In the Church of South India unique agreements were made in 1947 where churches with differing understandings of *episkope*, were able to give their consent to a unity scheme which was thought to be a possible model for others in former areas of separate missionary endeavour.

The *Charta Oeumenica*

In April 2001 the *Charta Oeumenica* was published by the Conference of European Churches (CEC) and the Roman Catholic Council for European Bishops' Conferences (CCEE). It pledges commitment to unity and action in facing common issues of peace and justice in Europe. Its basic standpoint is that the churches together have a commission as the founding part of the 'One Holy Catholic and Apostolic Church' to develop a 'common responsibility in Europe'. It is the nature of what they call apostolicity which provides the grounds and justification for activity. This apostolicity flows from a common understanding that the churches share oversight or *episkope* for the communities in which they are set, from which they derive their identity and in which they serve or minister. A bishop's identity derives from the place where the ministry is exercised and their work arises from the needs and activities of that community. The ministry is personal but also communal. The word *koinonia* is used in the commentary to the *Charta Oecumenica* to explore what it means to live 'in fellowship' as different churches/denominations and to live among the range of people served.

This European agreement marks a major step forward in common approaches to a number of issues. The agreement to act with a concerted approach to issues of peace and justice is a fundamental and significant starting place. It means that there can be major ecumenical stances on some of the great problems which face the people of all faiths and none in Europe. What is equally important is that the justification for this activity is the understanding that the churches share a common responsibility for the oversight of the many communities which make up the European continent. Key words whose meaning has been forged in previous agreements come here to be used with a common understanding, *episkope* and *koinonia* being significant among them. It then rests on those who are chosen and called to give leadership and to provide oversight which will put this and other agreements into practice.

An Anglican Covenant?

The hint at provincial autonomy mentioned in the Church of England House of Bishops' response to *Ut Unum Sint* has become a reality. The greatest challenge to the integrity of leadership as oversight in the Anglican Communion is the current situation concerning the fragmentation of dioceses and provinces.

Such a situation raises a fundamental question, one which is central to the exploration and argument which forms the subtitle of this book: how is a new model for episcopal leadership to be devised and exercised? Some basic assumptions are being challenged in this reinvention. These are about coherence and unity, about the exercise of *episkope* being a focus for unity and the place where doctrine is guarded and teaching given. Without a basic sense of unity and a will for differing groups to stay together, in what way can an episcopal church justify its existence? From the days of the early church to the rational justification of episcopal leadership by Richard Hooker, there has been a core agreement that allegiance to bishops is given by the people they have been chosen to serve. There certainly have been times when episcopal leadership has needed reform and when a different kind of person was needed to perform the task. There have been many calls for greater transparency in the ways in which leaders who will share in the exercise of *episkope* are appointed. No longer do most of our leaders come from an élite ruling class with a common blood-line and education with others who exercise governance in a nation. At a time when there is an increasing confidence in the appointments processes, whether by election or by appointment, we have arrived at a time when there is a lack of confidence in those who exercise the task.

Part of the reason for this is the series of divisions which have fragmented episcopal churches in modern times. To some extent, approaches to differences and divisions over human sexuality, interpretations of the Bible or the ministry of women are culturally determined. There have always been different groups and differences of doctrine and in ecclesiology within episcopal churches and particularly in Anglicanism. The key issue for today in particular is how to exercise leadership and oversight within the divisions and disputes which threaten the break-up of the Anglican Communion.

Aware of the deep divisions emerging in the Anglican Church and aware of the approaching Lambeth Conference of all Anglican bishops in 2008, the Archbishop of Canterbury, The Most Rev Dr Rowan Williams began to take steps to prevent a deeper rift. In doing this and with the participation of bishops in the process which he commissioned, an emerging responsibility for corporate governance and oversight can begin to be named. Here Anglicanism is beginning to rediscover what *episkope* can and should really mean.

In October 2003 the Archbishop of Canterbury set up the Lambeth Commission. Its brief was 'to make recommendations to the Primates of the Anglican Communion on how to maintain the highest degree of communion possible'. The Commission was chaired by The Most Rev Robert Eames, Archbishop of Armagh and Primate of all Ireland. They produced what is called 'The Windsor Report' for discussion by the Primates in January and May of 2005. Sufficient assent was reached for work to carry on in what is called the 'Windsor Process', steered by a Continuation Group.

The Windsor Report suggests an 'Anglican Covenant' (paras 113–120) to which each province could respond and, with agreed revisions, could become accepted as a base document signifying the kind of agreement of fundamental issues of scripture, sexuality and church order to which all could give assent. This process was continued with work being done by a Covenant Design Group. The Lambeth Conference was not to be the place where a Covenant was debated and agreed but a place where deep listening took place. Work continues through a Ridley-Cambridge working group who in 2009 produced a draft of the Covenant. Work continues on its acceptance.

In this process we can observe an active and committed interplay between leadership and oversight. Clearly, an archbishop has a particular responsibility to 'oversee' the work and responsibilities of the bishops in a particular province of the Anglican Communion. The Archbishop of Canterbury has, by common consent and the authority of history, a responsibility to oversee the whole Communion. His initiative to reach a new form of agreement that will bind Anglican identity is a clear and distinct form of leadership. It is not leadership from the front with a set of solutions; it is leadership which recognizes the fundamental character of shared *episkope*. The process which he set in motion exemplifies in a classic way how governance should be exercised in such a devolved church, but one which needs to maintain its own kind of unity. Here is gradual change and adaptation guided and sometimes policed by the person with actual and representative authority. It is leadership exercised as oversight with the kind of encouragement that can also state and establish boundaries. Outcomes are by no means final in this international debate. What is clear, but not yet acknowledged, is that a living *episkope* is being discovered within this family of episcopal churches.

New directions in *episkope* for bishops

Traditionally bishops have had a See or diocese and the name of their See relates to the geographical area in which they reside. Dioceses vary enormously in size and the larger ones have been sub-divided.

In these instances the diocesan bishop delegates some powers and responsibilities to another bishop for what is called an Episcopal Area within the larger diocese. In dioceses without an episcopal area scheme, there are many instances where suffragan bishops have episcopal authority delegated to them in a legal way by the bishop of the diocese.

In the report *Called to be One* produced by Churches Together in England, this system of delegation and sub-division is called into question.[13] Episcopal churches are encouraged:

- To consider whether their dioceses are so large that it is difficult for the bishop to have a real pastoral relationship to all the people of the diocese, and in what sense he can be a leader in mission for all its centres of population.
- To consider how the roles of auxiliary, suffragan or assistant bishop fit with the church's basic understanding of the ministry of the church.
- To consider whether the size of the diocese is chosen more for administrative convenience than out of pastoral or missionary concern.

No arrangement at the moment is entirely successful. There is a strong case to be made that a bishop is a bishop is a bishop and that each one should have the personal, collegial and communal responsibilities which go with their title or See. This question has been answered over time by the creation of smaller dioceses out of some of the larger ones. The appointment of one or more suffragan bishops has been an attempt to solve the same problem. Whether the creation of further suffragans, and the reduction in additional workload on diocesans are appropriate answers will depend on a review of what a bishop in the twenty-first century should be expected to do. There will not be one complete answer to this, but the development of models of episcopal oversight and of leadership will go some way to providing an answer.

In what ways are bishops 'leaders'?

In what ways are bishops the ultimate leaders of their communities? This is a significant and very modern question. These, often characterized by legalities and synodical restrictions on the freedom of bishops to exercise individual authority and initiative, bishops do feel very hemmed in. Many bishops attempting to bring about change in their dioceses are acutely aware of this. They live with a perpetual dilemma. Some clergy and laity in the church look to the bishop as leader and expect direction and on occasions control. Others, probably now in the majority among committed church members and many clergy, expect to participate in the development of policy, to have some control and accountability of expenditure, and to get realistic feedback from their bishop about expectations for their work and about the quality of their performance.

In a clear and most helpful way the report BEM sets out the place of bishops in the church and which roles and functions they perform:

> Bishops preach the Word, preside at the sacraments, and administer discipline in such a way as to be representative pastoral ministers of oversight, continuity and unity in the Church. They have pastoral oversight of the area to which they are called. They serve the apostolicity and unity of the Church's teaching, worship and sacramental life. They have responsibility for leadership in the Church's mission. They relate the Christian community in their area to the wider Church, and the universal Church to their community. They, in communion with the presbyters and deacons and the whole community, are responsible for the orderly transfer of ministerial authority in the Church.[14]

There is a tension which will remain between the personal working out of a role as bishop in a locality and the joint exercise of *episkope* which a bishop shares with the staff and people of a diocese. Personality plays an enormous part in the way in which any bishop sets out their ministry. One part of the selection procedure, whether by appointment or election, may well be an attempt to match the needs of a particular diocese with the type of personality that will best carry out what is thought to be needed. All bishops have to have a public persona and one of the responsibilities of office is for them to use the opportunities which access to the media provide to maintain a credible place for Christianity and to contribute in appropriate ways to major areas of public debate.

Most bishops will have been appointed because they have skills in a particular area of work. Some will have technical knowledge gained through a previous career, or through their academic research in a subject other than theology which occupied their life and career development before they were ordained. Others will just know how to handle the media, be good at radio and television interviews and have natural or acquired skills as communicators. In each case, when a bishop represents their denomination using the media they represent the whole.

Collegiality is essential, as is corporate responsibility for agreements made within synods and at the times when bishops meet together in conference. The most important factor in the discussion of a public face for episcopal leadership is always to be aware of the danger of personality. It is all too easy to be deluded by the glamour and notoriety of publicity and in being under the media spotlight. Deep foundations of spirituality are required to prevent an inappropriate response to the opportunities which personality and public acclaim brings. Bishops never represent themselves and their opinions alone. They may represent a particular point of view within an ecclesiastical or secular debate. They always express opinions in public as a member of a group who can hold one another to accountability in a range of ways. That is why such an exploration of *episkope* is timely and necessary. It is why ecumenical and international agreements about the nature of episcopal churches and their leadership are essential.

New directions for leadership and oversight

Significant new ground has been broken by recent theological pieces of writing and with a series of ecumenical agreements. These lead to an emphasis on core concepts or models for episcopal leadership. New directions are emerging which rely on a basic structure for church life and order which give an understood shape within which renewal and development can take place. The essential form of the body remains the same and is created and recreated in an enduring way. The renewal of *episkope* is a fundamental way of unfolding the corporate aspects of our common life in a way that indicates where the wider community of the church bears responsibility and where the particular ministry of bishops and their colleagues is fundamental. We have seen from the Lima document (BEM) and the 'Porvoo Common Statement' and echoed in all others that the ministry of oversight is exercised personally, collegially and communally.

At this stage in our examination it is possible to begin to see what new directions are emerging for leadership and oversight in our episcopally structured churches. For the rest of this chapter we need to go on and give more detailed identification to these directions. The most significant feature of episcopal churches is that they have one agreed and universal means by which they can be in relation with one another. It follows from this that they should have an internationally acknowledged leadership structure. This primary feature is underpinned in an important way because it was the very first structure which emerged in the first decades and then centuries in the life of the church. Most important and even fundamental for our study is that this one concept of episcopacy has not been static but has developed and adapted itself according to both political and ecclesiastical circumstances through the centuries. Change is still taking place and it needs to be evaluated in order for robust and acceptable new adaptations for *episkope* to be digested. Fundamental to all changes is that they contribute to the building up of trust rather than reflect mistrust and division.

Our ecumenical documents have already given us some key words and concepts by which we can identify key characteristics of *episkope* for the future. These have been noted and sketched out and are now offered as the template for new directions in episcopacy, leadership and oversight:

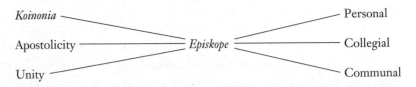

- *Koinonia* – every characteristic of *episkope* must arise from the community in which it is expressed. Christianity, while being a faith which upholds and inspires the individual, has alongside this the basic tenet that faith only grows and is informed by membership of a wider group, which itself is part of an even wider community.
- Apostolicity – the way in which this community of churches expresses its unity is that it adheres to internationally agreed characteristics and methods of appointment. Most significant of these is that the structure itself has transparent appointment systems which can be traced back to the work of the apostles, commissioned by Jesus, at the time of his earthly ministry. History is not everything and the nature and verification of 'apostolic succession' has been a great part of the agreements, and differences, in discussions about unity. The Porvoo Agreement has established this for the Scandinavian and Nordic Churches; the Anglican Communion has established this for its constituent churches and provinces; the Roman Catholic Church does not yet acknowledge this 'succession' as a basis for its unity with other churches. This lack of acknowledgement, and the emerging ways of giving pastoral oversight in a divided church, suggest that Apostolicity will take different forms as the search for a common mind and ecclesiology continues.

- Unity – uniformity and even structural coherence will not yet be the characteristic of episcopal churches. This is an affront to the concept, since the two characteristics described above have unity of ecclesiastical structure as the described basis for relationship. This absence does not mean that all is lost. It certainly describes the unfolding of history and the place at which episcopal churches find themselves in wrestling with contemporary disputes and issues.

The ecumenical documents have established some common and agreed ways to describe *episkope* as personal, collegial and communal:

- Personal – The very fact that *episkope* is expressed in the appointment of a person, a bishop, as the person who gives the oversight means that *episkope* will always be about people in relationship. It is the communities of the faithful who adopt this method of oversight or governance who acknowledge willingly that they do not exist in isolation: they are not independent, self-governing churches or communities. The style and nature of the personal nature of oversight is undergoing change. No longer will the monarchical style of episcopal leadership be acceptable in many or most parts of the world. Personal episcopal leadership and oversight will, as always, require the consent of the people who make up the church. From these communities will emerge, ready to be identified and called, those who have the qualities required for leadership and oversight of communities which have very different expectations from those of the first centuries or the Middle Ages. The pressures and new structures of the Reformation made new demands of churches which continued with episcopacy as a fundamental structure. It was the personal influence and example of the episcopal leaders of the day which built the bridges for a transition. Leadership is always personal, but always in relationship with other people, and is conducted in ways which reflect the needs and acceptable practices of an age.
- Collegial – The most significant characteristic of episcopally

led churches is that the leaders operate as a group in relation to one another. In order to teach agreed doctrines and to develop renewed missionary structures, bishops have to talk together, reach fundamental agreements together, and draw the boundaries of faith and order together. In order to do this, bishops have to represent their people as they meet together in provinces and as the provincial leaders, the archbishops, meet together in council. All this has now to be done in the essential relationship which bishops have with their clergy and their lay people as they meet together in synods. These structures were characteristic of church order in the first centuries and have now become an essential feature of modern church government. Such meetings are not the same as those expressed in most forms of modern democracy. The purpose of meeting in these groups is to debate together in attempts to achieve new solutions to contemporary issues. It is for the episcopal leaders, the bishops, to find their appropriate place in this modern system. It has to be a place which safeguards their historic and ecclesiastical role. Their new place will not be achieved, and gain consent, without their willingness to act collegially and represent the mind of a church which is universal in faith if not in structure. Trust is the key word, and it has to be won again through the willingness of bishops with differing views to work together in ways which aim to achieve a common mind on fundamental issues.

• Communal – Trust will not be achieved unless those expressing and exercising episcopal leadership represent changing expecta-tions and cultural norms in the societies in which they exercise their jurisdiction. Bishops represent tradition, and one of the characteristics by which they act with integrity is that they are aware of and are formed by their own tradition. Their ministry arises from the faith and the traditions of the communities which have shaped and chosen them. But 'communal' means much more than that today. Perhaps more than ever before communal authority contains within it expectations about accountability.

Never before have bishops needed to be accountable to their clergy and congregations in the ways that they are today. Authority is almost turned on its head and will be unless the ministry of *episkope* – oversight – has the consent of the people who are governed and cared for by bishops. These new expectations contain within them the emerging expectation that *episkope*, represented by one person, rests ultimately with the community which calls men and women out to be its leaders. This kind of communal oversight with representative figures who are vested with specific tasks and roles is unique to episcopal churches; it is a treasure which needs to be retained but is one which needs to be rediscovered and revalued by the communities of faith which give it shape and which owe it willing allegiance.

Transition or meltdown?

The changes in understandings of church life and the ministries of leadership and oversight we are describing are all about transition. They can all too easily feel like meltdown. Believe it or not, churches are good at transition. One of the partners in a particularly experienced consultancy company who work in both the public and private sectors has said that unlike many companies which undertook wholesale and sudden reconstruction, the gradual ways in which churches changed is a lesson in itself. We are not bad at everything we do or worse than those in others sectors of public life. In this area of gradual change and adaptation churches are often much better than many other companies or organizations. The noteworthy achievement of churches through the centuries is that they have undertaken considerable structural and cultural change and have been able to take the majority of members with them. This has been done by trusted leaders and reformers working with feelings and moods, and by introducing incremental change.

Those who like tidy solutions and clear, well-defined boundaries will find gradual transitional change very difficult. They will think that the old certainties, conveyed by tradition and clear teaching are ebbing away. Lovers of order and hierarchical authority will find today's churches confusing places. Much will be the same with new interpretations of episcopal governance. One difference in this case is that international agreements and the expectations of clergy and people in dioceses are ahead of the changes in work practice and attitude still in use by many bishops. Collegiality is not yet a main characteristic of episcopal life and decision making. Meltdown is a danger which can only be combated by the acknowledgement that certain changes have to be made if trust and credibility are to continue to be earned. Formation and re-formation are essential ongoing tasks in the relearning of the exercise of *episkope*.

It is clear from the descriptions and interpretations in this chapter that a number of fundamental and hard-won ecumenical agreements have been made. Some of these are in important areas where collaboration or collegial initiative could provide a springboard for further action. These have all the potential needed to provide a great impetus, but other things are required. No significant change will become established until certain behavioural characteristics come into play among present bishops and in those who will be inducted into the culture of episcopal leadership. For this to happen, and as a significant if not fundamental first step, some emerging models for *episkope* and episcopal leadership have to be established. Our journey has provided us with more than enough evidence. We now have to produce and sustain leaders who can bring into the life of our churches this renewed understanding of leadership and oversight. In the next chapter we must explore some of the spiritualities which can inform and protect those called to this essential work.

Notes

1 *Baptism, Eucharist and Ministry*, World Council of Churches, Faith and Order paper No 111. 1982.
2 Op. cit. p. 25, para. 24.

3 This is a summary of the argument on page 25, in section 24 of the BEM report.

4 *The Porvoo Common Statement*, Council for Christian Unity of the Church of England, Occasional Paper No 3. 1993.

5 *The Porvoo Common Statement*, p. 25. para. 44.

6 *2001 Common statement on Anglican-Methodist conversations*. p. 56, paras 185–90.

7 *The Sign we Give: a report from the Working party on Collaborative Ministry for the Bishops Conference of England and Wales*, 1995, p. 24.

8 *Catechism of the Catholic Church*, Geoffrey Chapman, 1994. pp. 204–6.

9 Church of England House of Bishop's reply to *Ut Unum Sint*, GS Misc. 495, p. 20.

10 See the debates between the Church of England and The Evangelical Church in Germany called the Meissen Commission, 1988. A commentary was published by the Church of England in 1997 as GS Misc. 490.

11 *Anglican-Methodist Unity*; The Scheme.

12 See *The Nature of Oversight: Leadership, Management and Governance in the Methodist Church in Great Britain* and *What is a District Chair?* Minutes of the Methodist Conference 2005.

13 *Called to be One*. p. 14, para. 2.33

14 B.E.M. p. 26, para. 29.

VIII

Spirituality and integrity

Those who undertake leadership tasks need to have significant spiritual resources. The work of a leader is for much of the time very public and frequently held under scrutiny. As a consequence of this the personality and actions of leaders appear magnified and receive attention and comment from a wide audience. It is now time to take a different approach in our examination of leadership and oversight. Without a spirituality which arises from a developed and reflective intellect – and one which is in some way apparent to others – a leader will be seen not to have the credibility and adequate resources to do the job. There is for every leader a close connection between their beliefs and values and their actions, however compromised these may seem on some occasions. That is why we need to explore what makes and sustains the spirit of a leader. In doing this I am making a close link between spirituality and values and the integrity which every leader needs to maintain as they make many difficult decisions.

In her novel *Ultimate Prizes*, Susan Howatch gives an interesting illustration of how she has observed bishops:

> In general there are two types of bishops: holy bishops and what I call chairman-of-the-board bishops. The latter are by nature businessmen with gregarious personalities and a flair for organization; their inevitable worldliness is mitigated by the spirit of Christ, and their success as bishops depends on the degree of mitigation. Holy bishops, on the other hand, usually have no talent for administration and need much time to themselves in order to maintain their spiritual gifts; their success as bishops depends less on the grace of God than on their willingness to delegate their administrative duties continually to talented assistants.[1]

This amusing comment reflects not only the public impact that leaders may make but also – and much more importantly – it points toward the checks and balances which leaders need to put in place to develop themselves and to pre-empt some of their failings. A spirituality which can support the responsibilities and challenges – and resist the temptations – of senior leadership needs to be developed.

St Bernard of Clairvaux, the Benedictine doctor and spiritual guide said, 'Everyone has to drink from his own well'.[2] This phrase was taken up by the Liberation Theologian Gustavo Gutierrez in his story of the spiritual journey of the people of Lima in Peru.[3] He contrasts the community experience of a people with the necessary solitude or space which an individual requires to keep their self-respect and to renew their spirit. The same need can be seen in any church leader whose public ministry requires them to take extra steps to resource themselves using a chosen spiritual tradition. For that resourcing to be earthed and invigorated by the everyday concerns of their people, they need to relate and draw their authority from the community that gives them their office. Their own personal discipline and self-awareness point again and again to their need for personal space and organized resources.

In secular life these needs are just as significant. Without reflection and renewal, any leader runs the risk of becoming empty or repetitive. A lack of self-awareness leads to the loss of the essential sensitivity which all leaders need in order to be able to know and be known by their people. A sense of detachment and even self-importance can grow as length in office continues. For these reasons it is always important for leaders to understand themselves and what drives them on. For some it is just hubris: the desire to push forward and create empires and focus power on themselves. For others it is the desire to serve or to achieve certain goals. While these remain paramount, then renewal and reflection – increases in self-knowledge – are possible. To take a completely secular example; at the end of his second book describing the astonishing characters he has met 'villains, spies, dictators and icons' in a lifetime of journalism and television presentation, John Simpson describes a link between our inner longings or aspirations and our public actions and achievements. He refers to Sir Thomas Browne, the seventeenth century physician who tried to map out and give reasons to explain his own spiritual journey: 'We carry within us the wonders we seek without'.[4]

What is it that the leaders of our churches and faith communities carry within them which needs to be sustained and developed as they exercise *episkope* and lead congregations and communities? We have already seen that Cardinal Basil Hume spoke and wrote about his need to spend time in 'the desert' in order to be resourced and equipped for his time in 'the market place'. He was not drawing solely on his own experience in making these remarks. His spirituality was drawn from the main well from which he had learned to drink as a Benedictine monk, and beyond that from the example of Jesus himself.

We know very well from each of the four gospels that Jesus took many opportunities to be away in a quiet place either by himself or with his disciples. These times always preceded events which would give him anxiety or which would make great demands on him. These 'desert' times began with the forty days and forty nights he spent in the wilderness before his public ministry began (Mt. 4.1–17). They ended with his prayers in the Garden of Gethsemane before his arrest, trial and crucifixion (Mt. 26.36–41). Such spiritual discipline underpins all Christian people and is expected of members of Religious Orders and of all Christian leaders. To make opportunities for reflection is an essential ingredient for having in place the supportive apparatus needed for those who take on stressful and responsible jobs. In order to be supported and kept to these disciplines, it is important to have a spiritual director, consultant or mentor.

Drinking from the well of tradition

Those who belong to and lead churches in the episcopal tradition do not begin with a clean sheet and the option to choose their own spirituality. In the Anglican tradition there is a basic pattern for all people to follow. This was created at the time of the Reformation and the compilation of the *Book of Common Prayer*. It was deliberately and aptly named. Constructed by Thomas Cranmer, Miles Coverdale and other reformers from the material gathered around and within the daily offices, it was designed for the lay person as much as for the cleric. Morning and evening prayer were constructed, with the Book of Psalms divided up so that there were daily prayers and readings for a 30-day month. In this way it was quite deliberately designed so that all could have a framework of accessible liturgical and biblical prayer to support, shape and resource them.

Alongside the daily offices went the discipline of regular attendance at Holy Communion. At first the injunction was to relatively infrequent attendance or celebration for most people. Spiritual traditions have developed so that a much more frequent celebration of communion has become the practice. Both the daily offices and the regular celebration of communion are linked very closely to the liturgical year. Church seasons and festivals are built in so that the complete range of human experience can be brought into a faith context and reflected on in the times and seasons of every year. For the minister and church leader, many of these events are linked with more public celebrations of the same events by infrequent church attenders and sometimes with those of other faiths.

What has been most important from the time of the establishment of this pattern of spirituality is firstly, for members of the Church of England and then for the churches of the Anglican Communion, that the fundamental doctrines and beliefs of the denomination are contained in their prayer books. This tradition and discipline has been continued through the various revisions to the present day. For the church leader this deliberate containing of the doctrine in the prayer books is particularly significant. Without regular use there is the possibility that essentials of the tradition and heritage of faith will not form an essential part of a minister's spirituality; it is the principal well from which a leader needs to continue to drink. With regular use the now internationally agreed liturgical texts and widely used common lectionary mean that a world-wide community is drawing from the same resource each day. It means that ministers and laypeople can meet and pray together with ease, ordinands can be selected and bishops and archbishops can meet, and whatever the difficult or contentious topic of their gathering, they can say their prayers together and experience a common bond of spirituality.

The reality of our modern international church is that not all ministers and not all senior leaders find this well of spiritual formation entirely sufficient. Many find that in busy lives a regular pattern of daily office, frequent celebrations of the eucharist, regular times for meditation and retreat and space for reading are not there. They replace these with less frequent prayer times and with refreshing additions from other traditions and other spiritualities. What is vital is that something is in place to provide added resources for a leader, and that some of these emerge from the tradition which they have been called to represent. When not firmly established in a life which is in some way organized and which has a planned pattern, then the opportunity for the distractions and illusions of office becomes much greater.

In terms of senior leaders we already know that there is not one kind of leader nor is there one kind of leadership. Leaders have different motivations and different personalities. Susan Howatch began us on this road with the light but well observed description of active 'chairman of the board' bishops and 'holy' bishops. She describes the wisdom, perhaps known better by their colleagues than by themselves, needed to exercise effective *episkope*. The same is true of the lifestyle or diary discipline of every leader. The over-active need to make times for reflection and to learn to listen to their colleagues, while those inclined to prayerfulness and introspection need immersion into a range of different situations and experiences to inform their study and enrich their prayer life.

The well of Benedictine spirituality

It is the spirituality of the Benedictine tradition which has captured the imagination and met the needs of many leaders in recent times. Pressurized businesspeople and church leaders who need to find some space outside the public arena to make sense of their lives have found the Benedictine balanced life of prayer and work speaks to their needs. St Bernard of Clairvaux found it was the well from which he drank. It is the place where Cardinal Basil Hume found his 'desert' and 'market place' image. He was in part drawing the example from the life and ministry of Jesus Christ as interpreted by St Benedict.[5] The Benedictine Rule was designed for those who wanted to live the religious life in community, but was deliberately designed to be accessible to all. Its attractiveness for many is that it involves a balance of life and work and has a regime of prayer and study which insisted on 'nothing harsh nothing burdensome' but which drew on the experiences which came from the ordinary experiences of life. Its appropriateness and significance for our study is that it regards relationships within the community as material for the sanctification of the whole. In this way the Rule of St Benedict is challenging or even counter-cultural in that it does not thrive on competitiveness and the reconciliation of difference but on mutual respect and accountability.

The Rule is designed to be lived within a settled community which works at achieving stability through the balancing of difference. For the leader, and especially for the church leader, there are some significant features which support them. We have already seen that there is a long history of identifying a bishop, archdeacon or dean with a particular geographical community. Leadership is almost always in relation to others in a work or geographic setting. This becomes important and sensible, since one of the big questions of our day is about how different groups and factions learn to live together in community. Speaking about Benedictine Spirituality in a lecture at Trinity Church, Wall Street in New York, Archbishop Rowan Williams pointed out that the chapters in the Rule on the Abbot's ministry emphasize that the place and work of the person in authority is not to mediate between fixed groupings of people or opinions but to 'attend to the needs and strengths of each in such a way as to lead them forward harmoniously'.[6] That is precisely the kind of attitude needed to exercise responsible *episkope*. It does not necessarily come naturally but emerges from the rhythms of a life shaped by the kind of prayerful discipline which helps understanding of what work in community is for and the purposes it can be designed to achieve.

The well of Franciscan spirituality

Identifying a different need and feeding the resources of many others in senior leadership positions is the spirituality of St Francis. The growth of the Third Order of the Society of St Francis, mainly made up of lay people but with some priests and bishops, is one of the new features of our religious life.[7]

Francis began his reforming work from quite a different perspective. He was frustrated by the church as he saw it. The son of a wealthy cloth merchant, he became convinced that radical reforms were needed in the way the church presented the gospel. From his original vision or conversion experience in the church of San Damiano in Assisi, he set out on a lifetime mission to rebuild the church. Attractive to many today is his desire to tell the gospel stories in new and creative ways. He wanted the parables acted out, often in the streets. We almost all know that it was Francis who created the Christmas crib in the form we use it today.

Of importance to the church leader are the approaches which Francis took to wealth and to the natural order. He was severely critical of the amassing of great wealth. As a result he did not want his followers to have any possessions. In doing this he challenges modern leaders to produce a critique of the ownership of property and the use of financial wealth. Church leaders who make visits to large industrial complexes, or who have to make statements about financial crises of one kind or another, can have another starting place from the common assumptions of an acquisitive society on which to base their own thinking. It begins for many with an exploration of the attitude of Francis and his followers to money. He spoke of Lady Poverty and, in a different way from the mainstream Christian or Jewish attitudes to wealth, saw dignity in the state of voluntarily possessing little or nothing.

Attractive to many is the way in which Francis embraced the created order. He was much more than a lover of birds and flowers; he spoke of 'brother' sun and 'sister' moon and in this revolutionary way established a new and very real personal relationship with the created order.[8] Church leaders are pressed today in many ways to lead by example in conservation matters. It is vitally important that they do so with a basis in theology and spirituality rather than in seeming to follow a current fashion.

A number of significant church leaders in modern times have been influenced by the spirituality and teaching or Principles of St Francis. Archbishop Desmond Tutu is one of many senior people who are members of the Third Order of St Francis. Bishop John Taylor says

of his discovery of the Franciscan tradition that it released the part
of Desmond which is a 'troubadour fighter'. For those Christians in
secular leadership, the Christian Association of Business Executives
(CABE) has taken the Principles of St Francis and turned them into
daily exercises over a month for those who want practical application
of Christian teaching as understood and interpreted by St Francis in
their everyday life.[9]

Spirituality and self-awareness

The purpose of a well-nurtured spirituality in a church leader has
another dimension from solely that of a personal discipline. It is
the essential element in ensuring that self-awareness is part of the
leader's kit-bag of essential tools. Separation from the colleagueship
of others is the burden of the leader. The longer a person is in post
the more they can run the risk of not being able to take advice and
listen to the critical friends around them.

To drink from the well of a well-formed spiritual discipline is
essential in the life and wellbeing of every leader. Spirituality, like
many other positive qualities, is known as much in the breach as in
the observance. No-one can say 'I am a very spiritual person' or even
'I lead in this particular way because of my underlying spirituality'. It
is for others to say, notice and affirm these qualities. When they are
not there, the lack of resources for the demands of the many tasks
pull a leader down and they suffer within themselves. When those
qualities are not there it becomes too evident that a person has *only*
reached their present position through experience and intuition, and
the fuel is running out. These leaders turn to solutions which have
worked for them in the past and use many anecdotes about previous
posts, parishes or dioceses where they have worked. An absence of
deep resources for the tasks of the present can be masked by a retreat
from reality or by too much humour and too many stories. Such
people can be very entertaining and certainly most personable, but
as leaders they are not travelling with their people to any new place.

Isolation and the temptation to self-aggrandizement

Every leader will complain about the necessary sense of isolation which goes with the job and its responsibilities. To some extent this is accurate, but in many ways creating distance which leads to isolation can be a deliberate role construction. This is often compounded by collusion between leaders who want to feel that they are 'different' and followers or staff who want to keep responsibility and the accountability which goes with leadership at arm's length. Particularly in church appointments, hubris – the tendency towards exaggerated self importance – can come with long service and long and unchallengeable senior appointments.

Dr David Owen, a former senior British politician and medical practitioner, has made an international study of the effects of long periods in power of some political leaders.[10] Sadly he does not extend this to senior church leaders, but many of the characteristics he describes can be recognized. One of the different features of senior leadership in the churches is that most are in the same post for more than seven and sometimes more than ten years. This contrasts with many senior managers in industry and commerce whose tenure is likely to be less than five years. Head teachers now have the same time frame for their work, and the pressures mean that many of them will be in post for less than seven years. Because church leaders will be in post for longer than most of their senior colleagues, they will be more susceptible to certain describable characteristics or temptations arising from the isolation of their situation. It is possible to associate the succumbing to a number of these temptations to a lack of a structure for personal discipline and spiritual self-awareness. It is the leader, and especially the faith leader, who needs to be well aware of the lifestyle and factors contributing to self-aggrandizement which can affect and change them. They need to take deliberate steps to prevent the onset or deepening of this behaviour.

From a long list, David Owen offers these symptoms which can be characteristic of leaders inside or outside the churches:

- a narcissistic propensity to see the world primarily as an area in which they can exercise power and seek glory rather than as a place with problems that need approaching in a pragmatic and non-self-referential manner
- a predisposition to take actions which seem likely to cast them in a good light
- a disproportionate concern with image and presentation
- excessive confidence in their own judgement and a contempt for the advice or criticism of others
- loss of contact with reality, often associated with progressive isolation
- a tendency to allow their 'broad vision', especially about the rectitude of a proposed course of action, to obviate the need to consider other aspects of it, such as its practicality, cost and the possibility of unwanted outcomes[11]

I would add another in the light of new leadership language and the development of other criteria to judge success:

- obsessive concern to achieve regardless of the cost and of other opinions in order to establish their own 'legacy'

Very interestingly, the medically trained Dr David Owen does not 'diagnose' the hubris syndrome as an inherent personality disorder in leaders but as an obsessive behaviour characteristic caused by long stays in positions of leadership and thus of power, with little external constraint on their actions. Persons surrounded by deference and who are at the top of a hierarchy are inevitably prone to this syndrome. They can succumb to the temptations of power or they can choose to rely only on a well-constructed system of external reference and spiritual direction to prevent them from the worst side of themselves – and perhaps of almost all of us.

Paul Tillich dwells in some detail on hubris in the second volume of his *Systematic Theology*. He regards hubris as the ultimate

estrangement of a person from God. This is in contrast to understanding all semblances of greatness as a small part of the greatness,
dignity and being of all who are made in the image of God. The
person with significant hubris sees themselves as the centre of their
world and their own self-aggrandizement as the purpose of their
work and the object of their privileged position:

> Hubris has been called the 'spiritual sin', and all other forms of
> sin have been derived from it, even the sensual ones. Hubris is not
> one form of sin beside others. It is sin in its total form, namely,
> the other side of unbelief or man's turning away from the divine
> centre to which he belongs. It is turning towards one's self as the
> centre of one's self and one's world.[12]

Tillich's theological analysis combines elements of Greek tragedy,
where heroes try to make themselves like the gods, with biblical
examples. Their failure to resist temptation condemns them to
be fallible human beings, 'the mortals' who condemn themselves
because they succumbed to the temptation to make themselves
like the gods, 'the immortals'. True Greek heroes are those who do
not succumb to the sin of hubris but resist it and thus show their
greatness. It is this that makes them stand out from the ordinary and
the all too fallible.

Tillich moves immediately to the first and greatest biblical
example at the very beginning of the book of Genesis. Here Adam
and Eve are tempted through the serpent's promise that if they eat of
the tree of knowledge they will become equal to God. He sees also
one of the roles of the prophets as challenging kings and the powerful
for the misuse and abuse of power, caused by elevating themselves to
become like God rather than remembering to retain their humility
and being all too aware of their fallibility and the fragility of their
position.

It is a particular characteristic of being a bishop that a sense of
distance from others in the church seems to become established all
too easily. The whole lifestyle, dress and place in the liturgy appear

to symbolize the different rather that the collegial nature of a team of senior clergy and lay people. These characteristics, along with the secular pressure to cast the bishop as the managing director or chief executive, suggest hierarchy and separation rather than co-operation or collaboration in the life of a church. Each conspires together to isolate the humble or self-aware and to feed any latent sense of self-importance which may be waiting in the shadows. They are the enemy of collegiality. It is said of the former Bishop of Bradford, Roy Williamson, that he always insisted that he walked in *with* his senior staff at all diocesan services and events to emphasize the collegial nature of their work.

It is the interaction between a leader and their team or leaders and followers which gives life or essence to leadership. It is even more the case with oversight. Without a relationship of trust and respect, the oversight which a leader exercises is worthless. For this reason I am convinced that there is an essential link between a leader's values, a Christian leader's spirituality, and the integrity with which they make their decisions and the respect which they are accorded by their communities. Women and men who have become leaders know that to be true. In order to reflect in this way any leader will have shown some promise, had the confidence to face a range of tasks and, in all likelihood, ended up with a feeling that they might have done better. That is perhaps as good an expression of self-awareness as might be expected from an experienced but battle-worn leader.

Leadership and integrity

I now want to make a leap which I think is a logical one from the insistence that any leader needs to be aware of the values which drive them to the conclusion that their actions and decisions draw their integrity from their values. In any event self-awareness and integrity go together. The meaning of the word integrity is important for us as it is one of the key requisites which commands respect and loyalty between leaders and led. Integrity can mean 'wholeness, soundness, uprightness, honesty'. It can mean 'complete by the integration of parts into a whole, to make whole or to be undivided'. There is a bridge between spirituality and integrity which deliberately creates a place where the integration of ideas and experience can take place. This is the realm of reasoning which is learned through the maintenance of rigorous intellectual practice.

Richard Higginson, Director of the Ridley Hall Foundation for the Study of Faith in Business, is someone who has studied integrity as part of his analysis of the nature and quality of leadership.[13] He points out that integrity is a word which appears in a wide range of mission statements produced by commercial companies; the examples he has found are in those from Cadbury-Schweppes, National Westminster Bank, the Ford Motor Company, British Petroleum, Shell, Hewlett-Packard, United Biscuits and British Aerospace. This must give the concept some contemporary significance in the world of corporate ethics and has to have a particular relevance as a characteristic of ecclesiastical leadership. He also points out that throughout the Bible, and particularly in the Book of Job and the Book of Psalms it is used to describe 'righteousness' and 'uprightness'. (Job 2.3, 2.9, 27.5, 31.6, Ps. 7.8, 25.21, 26.1)

Not surprisingly, integrity is a persistent and attractive 'virtue' in the Book of Proverbs:

> The integrity of the upright guides them, but the crookedness of the treacherous destroys them. (11.3)
> Better is a poor man who walks in his integrity than a man who is perverse in speech and is a fool. (19.1)

Higginson concludes that such frequent use of integrity implies certain expectations of the senior leader and of the public or socially responsible company. These characteristics include fair dealing, vigilance over standards and about safety and honesty in dealing with others. He decides each of these combine to build up trust and to give credibility both to the actions of a person and also to the organization for which they are responsible.

Integrity in faith leaders might be expected or even assumed. That is not always the case and respect has to be won, often over and over again as difficult decisions have to be made. No-one coming into office can assume that the inherited qualities of their predecessors will automatically be assumed of or conferred on them. Credibility and trust have to be earned. They require experience fed by spirituality and by intellect.

Streams of spirituality

In a piece of research commissioned by the Foundation for Church Leadership in 2005 for their inaugural conference, and published as *Focus on Leadership*,[14] Stephen Croft used the analogy of 'the mine' rather than the well to describe the place where resources for leadership and the equipment for leadership can be found from Moses to the present day. The way in which the Church has structured itself, he concludes, is such that all God's people, through the commitment made in their baptism, are actively engaged in all its ministries. He develops his theological position by describing how he sees *episkope*, the ministry of oversight, as having four distinctive roles:

- watching over yourself
- building, guarding and guiding a missionary community
- enabling the ministry of others
- location, representation and connexion

These roles combine to be the essential ingredients of formation for responsibility which can create and sustain those called to ministries of oversight.

What is important is that any church leader should have some place or some places which act as a frame of reference for them. These can appropriately be described as 'the wells from which we drink'. Benedictine or Franciscan spiritualities are two of many. All arise from reading the scriptural texts as a basic discipline. The denominational tradition, whether Anglican, Methodist, Baptist,

Lutheran or Roman Catholic, needs to inform the spirituality of church leaders perhaps more than others, since they are called to represent this tradition to their people. Some of the difficulties for church leaders today can be traced to the difference between their choice or experience of a tradition which is not the main one which forms their denominational base and in which they are leaders. Most types of spirituality will transcend denominational boundaries. Indeed, all that have vitality and speak to a common religious need will do so. In this way Celtic spirituality and the outworking of faith from the Iona Community have influenced many. In terms of peace and reconciliation, association with the Corrymeela Community in Northern Ireland has been a source of spirituality and reconciliation. There are now Christian leaders who also look to other faith traditions to feed and inform their spiritual journeys. To be a leader without a very real and developing spirituality is to face extreme vulnerability. The market place and the desert are the life-blood of every leader struggling to retain their integrity and lead with a divinely-guided sense of purpose.

Notes

1 Howatch, Susan. *Ultimate Prizes*, Collins, London 1989.
2 *Bibet de fonte putei sui ipse*. St Bernard of Clairvaux. De consideratione.
3 Gutierrez, Gustavo, *We drink from our own wells*, SCM, 1984.
4 Sir Thomas Browne, *Religio Medici*, 1643. Quoted by John Simpson in *Mad World my Masters*, Pan, 2001, p. 415.
5 For the Rule see: www.osb.org/rb/
6 Rowan Williams, Archbishop of Canterbury, Lecture at Trinity Church, Wall Street, New York, 29 April 2003, 'God's Workshop'. Part of the Shaping Holy Lives conference on Benedictine Spirituality.
7 The Third Order has grown from 300 to 3,000+ in the U.K. in the years 1995–2009.

8　See *The canticle of the Sun* composed by St Francis.

9　See CABE Principles for Business, 2006. www.principlesfor business.com

10　Owen, David, *The Hubris Syndrome: Bush Blair and the intoxication of power*, Politicos, Methuen, 2007.

11　Op.cit. p. 1,2. He has followed this with a more extended survey of many other political leaders in *In sickness and in health: illness in heads of government during the last 100 years*. Methuen. 2009.

12　Tillich, Paul, *Systematic Theology*, Vol. 2. James Nisbett & Co, 1964, pp. 56–9.

13　Higginson, Richard. *Transforming Leadership: A Christian Approach to Management*. SPCK, 1996, pp. 54–8.

14　Croft, Steven, *Focus on Leadership*, Foundation for Church Leadership, 2005.

IX

The DNA of an emerging church

When I began this exploration of leadership and oversight I set myself a clear objective. This was to try to understand why concepts of collaborative leadership had not taken root in the episcopal churches. Mine was initially a pragmatic search born from a career trying to encourage many people in different parts of the church to discover or understand the motives and values which informed their work. It was also a quest for the ways in which church leaders from bishops to parish priests could develop a new understanding of how they could work together and become more trustful. I was looking for ways to encourage more collaboration and for a language based in theology to inform and encourage this search. I knew that the church had changed in many ways since I set out on the path to ordination and that many of today's church leaders were coming from different places and saw things in different ways. I had not realized until I was moving towards the completion of this in-depth study that my thinking would be taken to some very different places. The work came to represent much more than a personal journey for me. It gradually began to take the form of an exploration into what it is which could hold together episcopal churches within and beyond their local boundaries. Through an initial description of the vacuums in the life of our churches I came to see that what was needed was not more on improving the quality of our leadership; it was an exploration of what it was that could make us *want* to feel responsible for one another. I saw that this required a rehabilitation of the uses and meanings in a church context of leadership and oversight.

It became clear to me that the solution was to be found in a renewal of the memory of what it is that gives meaning and identity to churches with episcopacy as an essential part of their make-up. In order to plumb the depths of the possible core meanings of episcopacy it has been necessary to enquire where the concept came from and why it has endured, and been guarded so jealously, through so many generations. In a number of comparative examinations of the governance of episcopal churches I have found myself led to examine the emergence of descriptions or models for how oversight is required, hoped for and much needed in the different places where shared responsibility is the only alternative to fragmentation or schism. At the end of this study I have come to see that a deeper understanding of what it means to belong to an episcopal family of churches could well be the key to a fundamental dilemma: how to fill the vacuum of coherence and bring an end to the lack of goodwill which exists to find mutually owned solutions. It is no exaggeration to say that such a discovery could point us to the DNA, the essential character and structure of all episcopal churches.

A new and richer journey

Changes in my own thinking would have been one thing and could well have produced some challenging conclusions. But the church around the world has been changed by many controversial events even in the time that I have been writing. Episcopally led churches have been challenged by cultural and ethical issues which have produced a range of differing responses. Internally churches which up until now have been held together by membership of a common international family have been fractured by separatist movements. Bishops and archbishops who once were the people symbolizing a church which was One, Holy, Catholic and Apostolic have ceased in many cases to be the focus for unity and oneness and have become leaders of disaffected groupings. These very public and international differences have shown to the world, and to the local membership of churches, a picture of fundamental division and a leadership caught up in and sometimes expected to represent positions of difference.

This situation is not one which can be attributed to post-modernism where there is a general mistrust of authority and where there is a belief that our flawed leaders cannot really deliver us from anything. Mine is a conclusion which has been reached after an analysis of what episcopal churches are like. It comes after an extensive look at the presuppositions or models by which church leaders shape their lives and their activities. It has come after a long look at how leadership is viewed 'from the pew' and 'from the market place'. Most interestingly, and most soberingly, my conclusions have come after a look at the principal ecumenical documents and agree-ments of the last decades where, after baptism and other fundamental membership tenets, episcopacy as a collegial concept has featured as a significant source of agreement. This appears to be in contrast to a quite different and dissonant practice of episcopacy in many cases by those appointed to these pivotal positions.

An analysis of the systems which appoint leaders in episcopal churches has found that while there has been an enormous focus on greater transparency in the methods of appointment, there is no analysis of the essence of episcopacy which newly appointed people are expected to understand or become inducted into. In an equally stunning discovery there is little or no systematic way in which potential leaders are given appropriate professional devel-opment to allow their formation to be such that they move through a system which will nurture them as suitable for senior leadership appointments. There is no organized way of identifying and testing out people who through their existing practice demonstrate that enabling ministries of leadership are their preferred or even natural leadership styles.

Hidden treasure

This catalogue of negative findings, however formative for me, has not become a list of complaints leading to the conclusion of a book which is laden with doom. These findings have presented a number of achievable solutions. All are about the present and future shape or shapes of the Church. They lead to new possibilities in the practice of *episkope*.

It is probable that episcopally led churches are going to become more diverse and exclusive in their nature than ever before. Our differences are out in the open for all to see. They are not differences caused by the tensions of internal church fashion or liturgical window dressing. The differences are of an international kind. They are about fundamental matters of principle. Leaders represent difference and have a constituency of followers. They are no longer figureheads in a church held together by consensus, loyalty and an unspoken sense of shared identity.

What has gone wrong seems to me now to be an obvious loss. It is a loss which has come about by default. We have not been conscious of what we are doing. Our differences and divisions, in such stark contrast to our theoretical or theological agreements, can mean only one thing. It is that we have lost sight of the one concept which we say gives us our identity and which holds us together. The jewel of understanding about a shared responsibility for our church life expressed as *episkope* or oversight has become completely obscured. By stirring up so much dust through enjoyment of our controversies, we have managed to cloud or even bury the treasure which we once guarded so preciously from the time when our church was begun and as it has gone through so many other changes through the centuries.

The renewed kind of *episkope* which combines oversight with leadership will have to be grown and nurtured over a significant period of time. We have seen in many places through this study that one of the unrecognized strengths of episcopal churches is that they change by gradual adaptation. Under-researched and under-evaluated change has been taking place. Its consequence has been to produce a disjointed church with no coherent philosophy of how it works, why it is making the decisions it makes and what the best processes are for producing the kinds of consensus that will build lasting change.

The adding together of these individual conclusions lead to my basic question about *episkope* and episcopal leadership: how have we lost the memory of the culture which gave us birth? It seems that we no longer own a shared belief that the mutual oversight of our churches is the spirit-given treasure which has been our defining characteristic. We have now to begin the long process of adaptation or rediscovery which will build trust and give a corporate and more widely owned sense that we want to belong together in this church and to make a new journey. I have tried to make my own contribution by answering for myself a series of questions. I hope that they will at the very least inform and provoke more debate. As members of the family of episcopal churches we share a responsibility together to change and reshape our culture. We can only lead by example. The questions to which answers have now been found in this study are these:

- what are the core tasks of *episkope*?
- how can more effective leaders emerge and be developed?
- how can parish clergy share in *episkope*?
- can appointments systems be made more credible?
- can our leaders reform structures and systems?
- what would build a culture of trust?

What are the core tasks of *episkope*?

Can the core tasks of *episkope* be recovered? The alternative, which is a real and alarming possibility, is that *episkope* has a continuing but devalued status as an idea which holds together and represents particular groupings which are led by bishops within a denomination. The present situation may be a transitional one which will result in a new kind of coherence and unity, but we are not yet in a place where this can be seen. One important way forward could be that bishops who represent difference can choose the role of pontifex and find ways to keep open or to create the bridges over which people can cross to exchange experiences and to find new ways to travel forward together. For this situation to come about, some theology and some strategic tasks need to be established.

The first core task of *episkope* is to give coherence to belief in a credible and acceptable way. Integrity itself means bringing together different strands into an integrated whole. Theologians are the thought leaders who do the greatest part of this work. In the opening paragraph of his major work of systematic theology, John Macquarrie, Professor at Union Theological Seminary in New York, stands in the tradition of significant twentieth-century theologians. More a systematic interpreter than a ground-breaking innovator, he brings perspective to the theological disputes of our day. In this he acknowledges his particular indebtedness to Barth, Brunner and Tillich but particularly to the Roman Catholic theologian Karl Rahner and his colleague at Union, Professor John Knox. Macquarrie states the role and task of the theologian in a bold way:

> Christian theology seeks to think the Church's faith as a coherent whole. It aims not only at showing the internal coherence of the Christian faith, that is to say, how the several doctrines constitute a unity, but also at exhibiting the coherence of this faith with the many beliefs and attitudes to which we are committed in the modern world. Only if these tasks are accomplished can the faith be held intelligently and be integrated with the whole range of human life. The theological task needs to be done over and over again, as new problems, new situations, and new knowledge come along.[1]

Macquarrie was writing in 1966 in what can seem like a different age. He was prophetic in stating that the challenge to bring coherence was not a once-for-all task which can be accomplished in a series of influential and formative books. He knew that it would be a perennial task, required to renew both church and society. It was the continuation of a stream of ecclesiastical thought that was characterized by William Temple, himself a philosophical theologian: that the task of the Christian leader, and the place for them in the church and in wider society, was to contribute coherence of thought and experience by bringing their values and belief to bear on contemporary issues. Their role in public life was to give a series of leads towards a greater sense that society as well as the church would be better if bridges were built and a mutuality of understanding achieved. We have seen earlier in this book that Bishop Michael Adie came to a similar conclusion when he reflected on many years supporting episcopal ministry and then when a busy bishop himself.

Macquarrie develops his integrated theology in a way which culminates with clearly stated views on ministry and mission, and the place of episcopal leadership. He is certain that the principal role of lay people is the work of service and witness in the world, and that the work of the diaconate and the priesthood is that of pastoral witness and service. The task of the episcopate, he says, is twofold:

> It is the culmination of the ministries of the laity and of the ordained deacons and priests. The function of episcopal ministry is to represent the church as a whole as a united and coherent structure. But *episkope* has a particular challenge; this is to bring different groups and theologies together into this wholeness through a ministry of reconciliation.[2]

This is done, Macquarrie believes, through what is more than a *via media* – a middle way. It is done through holding in tension extreme positions, both in church and in society, utilizing 'a kind of dialectic which operates throughout history'. This is the task both of leadership and of *episkope* as it works with the tensions and challenges that repeat themselves in each situation of change.

The second core task of *episkope* is to prevent further division and begin to build a church based on shared trust and accountability. Macquarrie holds that the task of episcopal leadership is to exercise a ministry of reconciliation. It embraces both servant leadership and the belief that resurrection – the opening up or revealing of new ways forward – is of the essence of spirit-led *episkope*. He sees the culmination of ministry and of mission as the work of reconciliation, which is both Christ-like and of the essence of the theology which St Paul develops of the work of God in the death and resurrection of Jesus Christ. He understands the task of reconciliation, given to all but which reaches its culmination in the work of *episkope*, as the continuation of the work of Creation:

> By 'reconciliation' is meant the activity whereby disorders of existence are healed, its imbalances redressed, its aliena-tions bridged over. Reconciliation in turn is continuous with consummation, the bringing of creation to perfection. Creation, reconciliation and consummation are not three successive activ-ities of God, still less could we think that he has to engage in reconciliation because creation was unsuccessful. ... Creation, reconciliation and consummation are not separate acts but only distinguishable aspects of one awe-inspiring movement of God – his love or letting-be, whereby he confers, sustains and perfects the being of his creatures.[3]

The great danger in a church which is becoming characterized and defined by its differences is that many good people will choose not to participate. This is the greatest threat to the existence for the future of churches which claim to be open to all. Many will feel there is not a place for them and that the inclusiveness inherent in episcopal churches is no longer present. Enormous amounts of energy are expended on internal disputes which add nothing to the greater good of society and do nothing to model tolerance and inclusiveness.

Equally significant for models of leadership is that faith leaders are not demonstrating a significantly different way which gives a sense of unity around new and developing senses of direction. Instead we see episcopal leaders acting more like a drawbridge putting up defences which reinforce difference, rather than acting in the historically acknowledged role of bridge builder for people who need a particular kind of leadership at a specific time to create a way forward from a particular impasse.

The exercise of *episkope* that represents and reinforces difference or seeks to establish permanent division in the Church falls far short of this divine command and work of perpetual reconciliation. This work began at Creation but finds its deepest interpretation in the purpose of the sending of Jesus who is the Christ. It has to be confirmed in the work of the leaders in the church whose task is to sustain, guard and nurture the Body of Christ and be leaders in its work of reconciliation. The deliberate choice to work together will be the beginning of a rediscovery of the core tasks of *episkope*.

What kind of oversight will confident local churches accept?

The newest feature of churchgoing in the western world is that congregations are now made up of much more committed people who have a more thought through faith and a significant financial stake in the life of their local church. This means that they expect a greater say in the local and sometimes regional or national organization of their church. No longer can senior staff make appointments and decisions about deployment of clergy in a unilateral way. Equally, in very many places congregations can no longer have the level of care and cover from their own individual stipendiary/paid clergy that has been the nature of the local church for centuries. This different situation requires new thinking and consultation over ways forward. Underlying this it requires a new kind of relationship between the local church and its diocesan and national synodical representatives.

One obvious danger is that episcopal churches with confident congregations move their essential nature to becoming more like a collection of semi-competitive stallholders. Such a change would also reflect the growing liturgical and party differences between congregations. The principal consequence would be, or is already, that the nature of episcopal oversight would be diminished. Bishops and their senior staff would either always be required to try and oversee and lead groups and their clergy, some of whom disagree with them on fundamental matters of principle, or bishops become non-territorial, presiding over congregations who in effect 'choose' them. Neither of these positions could be recognized as legitimate in the structures and theology of a church which has as its fundamental tenet the acceptance of broad geographical episcopal oversight.

The types and models of oversight which confident congregations and those needing more support and affirmation will accept have three overarching characteristics. I call these organic, directional and authoritarian. It is my view that a wide acceptance of these would go some way to re-establishing relationships of trust. If the roles were understood and were carried out in effective ways they would gain assent from all but the most extreme among clergy and congregations. These ministries and roles would also give a clear steer about the kinds of people required when vacancies occur at any level and the nature of the training and formation which such embryonic leaders will need.

• Organic oversight: One of the basic precepts of Christianity is that its adherents should walk a spiritual path which takes them towards a greater sense of personal wholeness, growing in their understanding of themselves and of God. On this journey they will always be accompanied by others. This fundamental concept of personal development has to be reflected in the nature and quality of leadership in episcopal churches. Words which give immediate and strong mind pictures have been suggested. These include Gardener, Chef, Teacher and the well-rehearsed Servant. All these set out a basic theme that part of the role of those in authority is to create situations where people can grow, not only in spiritual awareness but also in their personal view of themselves called to discipleship in a particular place or area of work. Domineering leadership, unable to listen and empathize, will not reflect these qualities and will appear, and be, remote from the needs of many congregations and clergy.

- Directional oversight: Vibrant local congregations are by definition going somewhere. The energy which they have will be focused around a strong sense of purpose. Most often this is centred on a clear internal spirituality and an articulated sense that meeting needs in the community or supporting members in their sphere of work are essential activities. Such congregations will only respond to external interventions in their local life if these also suggest that they are strong and directional, and have been formed through careful listening to the needs of those in strategic local situations. Words used to describe this type of oversight in leadership are Navigator, Bridge Builder, Missioner, Pioneer, Interpreter and the widely accepted ecclesiastical image of Shepherd. Each of these requires a relationship which is two way. Most importantly, each of these concepts requires that trust is present.

- Authoritarian oversight: Everyone needs boundaries. This is particularly so in the case of religious belief and denominational identity. Leaders exercising oversight have to be steeped in the tradition which has formed them, and represent this by action and teaching to those in their care. Equally there have to be appointed leaders who exercise discipline. Structures and responsible officers within a denomination have to exercise discipline, and the archdeacons and bishops appointed have to exercise that authority on behalf of the whole church. Words such as Parent, Lawyer, Monarch and Legitimator are used to describe these essential functions. The authority of oversight also requires a relationship which is two way. Trust is essential if leaders need to exercise discipline on behalf of the whole church community.

It is not too flippant to say that 'saint' is the composite description for a person with these all qualities. We know, however, that our leaders are not saints and that they cannot carry out all these roles with their associated tasks themselves. This is the greatest practical argument for episcopacy as shared oversight. No one bishop in a diocese can do all these things, just as no clergyperson in a parish can carry out every activity. What leaders exercising oversight do is to embody and affirm each of these attributes and roles. The exercise and administration of them is a shared task. Confident congregations and well-briefed and supported clergy understand this. They take on some of these tasks of oversight themselves, they entrust others with some of the particular responsibilities and they expect their bishop to be the focus for the combined activity. It is only when clergy and congregations do not have the confidence both that they are trusted and that their leaders are carrying out tasks in the most effective ways that they begin to look for alternative networks and possibly alternative episcopal oversight.

How can more effective leaders emerge and be developed?

What is most surprising is that no integrated staff development functions exist across episcopal denominations. I have reviewed at some length the reports which have been produced in recent years. While all are designed to oil the wheels of senior appointments processes, none are designed to address the task of how a programme of staff development should be delivered, if indeed it is considered necessary at all. There is a stated need in each of the most significant reports to find ways of identifying those who might become available for selection to senior appointments. No structure is suggested in any place that I have been able to find which will look right across a province and provide training and development programmes for the type of clergy who can be seen as potentially suitable for greater responsibility. Without a personnel function or a staff development network, the prevailing culture of amateurism or of training provided by independent organizations will remain all that is on offer.

The biggest gap remains in the ineffectiveness of episcopal churches in identifying and developing potential future leaders. One incontrovertible reason for this is that there is very little clarity, and no worked through theology or ecclesiology, about what the job entails. Without a conscious understanding of the kind of oversight a church will need, it is hardly possible to develop training programmes and to identify potential candidates. Without a clear and well-negotiated role description of what the job is, it is hard to develop suitable candidates, and to decide against others.

So the answer to the question about how more effective leaders can be identified and developed has to begin with the response that we need a greater understanding of the ministries of oversight to which they will be called. This study is raising the questions and beginning to provide some of the answers. The gaping void continues, and will remain as long as individual interpretations are allowed to flourish and fill the vacuum produced when no-one is clear what leadership and oversight in the churches should look like.

First steps could or should be to review what is done internationally for senior leaders. A harvesting from the best of programmes in the different episcopal provinces will give a certain amount of infor-mation. More opportunities for senior leaders to meet as people with a particular responsibility and not for business reasons or as competitors would build a new atmosphere of trust. It is interesting to note that the Foundation for Church Leadership has begun some of this peer-sharing work in its own sensitive and discreet way. The establishment of any kind of international training programme for senior leaders needs to move from a pipe dream frustrated by ecclesiastical politics to a necessity which has to be promoted and adequately resourced. One national or international physical place for such a staff college is unlikely to be appropriate. But a 'virtual college' run by a network of training agencies and denominational officers is still a possibility. It has been suggested by many that initial training programmes in leadership should have been completed before a candidate can be considered for selection. The need for a well-resourced training and development arm is long overdue and is one of the gaping holes in the collective lack of care for our senior leaders. It could, and should, have an international dimension. Those preparing for episcopal ministry and those already in post would gain enormously from internationally developed resources, colleagueship and support.

How can parish clergy share in *episkope*?

If the work of *episkope* is only about the work of bishops, then this exploration will have failed to meet its objectives. The only way in which the concept of oversight will be returned to a central place is for it to become once again a way of belonging to a church that is shared by everyone. The particular role of leadership exercised as oversight is the privilege of those called to particular responsibilities. Those responsibilities are shared by all those who are called and ordained as priests as much as they are by those who are called and consecrated as bishops. The important difference is in an understanding of the particular work of oversight required from each.

Episkope expressed as the joint concept of leadership and oversight requires a subtle but essential set of ingredients. The first of these is the theological conviction that *episkope* is not the sole province of bishops, even working together in collegial groupings, but is a shared concept which stretches from bishop to parish priest and includes many lay people in positions of responsibility. The second is that it has an implicit acknowledgement that certain appointed leaders carry our particular roles and functions, on behalf of all the members. The third is that an international and publicly acknowledged commitment to shared *episkope* also provides an essential and key concept which can turn our churches round from places which focus only on the local and diocesan to places where membership of an international community becomes a reality.

The most important characteristic of episcopal churches is that they are more than congregational in nature. This goes against a prevailing and most natural trend. Episcopal churches are part of a family. Their ministry and indeed their identity arise from their being shaped by a relational link which is beyond the local. They acknowledge that each congregation is under the oversight of the grouping of parishes which make up a deanery, and that key responsibilities for both safeguarding tradition and teaching, as well as for the maintenance of buildings and finance, comes from a shared commitment to one another. The absence of this acknowledgement – or a festering resentment towards it – gives rise to many of the characteristics of modern episcopal congregations. They often behave as if they are in competition with one another in a locality. This sense of competitiveness or rivalry is compounded by a range of ecclesiastical traditions – high, catholic, liberal, evangelical, charismatic – which at the moment serve more to define difference than to embody a range and breadth of practice. Dioceses and diocesan offices are seen as a burden and the 'common purse' contribution to fund the overall costs of ministry as a form of taxation.

Clergy in episcopal churches are all ordained into an organization with a common understanding of itself. They are ordained into a church, founded on the ministry of Our Lord, the Apostles and Prophets, which is contained in the continuity of episcopal succession and the passing on of orders. In practice, Anglican clergy in many places appear to have lost sight of this common identity. They gravitate to groupings which are not always even within their denomination. So it is that Catholic clergy will look towards Roman Catholic and sometimes Orthodox clergy and congregations for their networking. Similarly, evangelical clergy will look towards colleagues in reformed or other evangelical churches, many of whom do not have anything of the same structure of liturgical worship and ecclesiology, some of which are in essence congregational in nature. These associations do prove that clergy and congregations look for colleagueship and for other partner congregations that will help them define their identity, but that they do not look to their parent denomination to be the principal source of this identity or to provide the still needed oversight. A fundamental core concept has been treated like an anachronism or as a no longer acceptable bond.

The theological and practical characteristic to bring energizing win-win attitudes is that episcopal communities need a well-defined and structured leadership just as much as they need sensitive oversight. This happens at a local level through colleagueship with the clergy, and at a diocesan level through the interaction of the bishop(s) and other staff with the synodical system. This joint work enables participative ministry and gives confidence for mission.

Can appointments systems be made more credible?

Lack of belief in the credibility and openness of appointment systems leads to low morale. It can also lead to unwillingness on the part of some able clergy to give of their best in the mature and experienced years of their ministry. We have seen that reviews of appointment systems can contribute much to the desire for trans-parency. Credibility requires more than an openness in the selection procedures; it requires a confidence that ability and suitability are the key criteria for selection of candidates. Since there is no widely accepted study and description of the tasks within the overall episcopal role, then there can be little confidence that procedural reforms will bring the much needed change. Appointment systems can only be credible, and believed in by those operating them, if it is known what people are being selected for, what they are supposed to do and what they might become as they grow into their calling.

We have been able to observe earlier in this study that a number of reviews have been completed which look at episcopal appointments in the Church of England. They have been carried out by those well versed in the way able people move into prominence in public life. There have been some detailed descriptions of the processes and some salutary and extremely clear sets of recommendations about how appointment systems might be worked more effectively. The question 'what for' has not been put, and consequently has not been answered.

Credibility comes when those doing the appointing understand and articulate what it is they are looking for in a next senior appointment. This can begin when a more focused understanding is developed. A new understanding of shared *episkope* will then define the work of bishops, archdeacons, cathedral deans and senior lay staff, as well as what is required of parish clergy. When this takes place there will be much less emphasis on the appointment of a personality and much more concern that shared responsibility for oversight will be filled by an appropriately described, prepared and selected candidate. It is equally important that the person appointed knows the process by which they were selected and the ethos of oversight into which they will be introduced and inducted. It can be hoped that the opening up of the debate in this book will begin to restore credibility. At the very least some searching questions have been asked.

Credibility will require much more than believing in a process of appointment that has been carried through in the clearest and most unbiased way possible, whether by election or by internal appointment. The testing of new ways for the development of *episkope* involves a mutual recognition that what is being done is happening with the consent and understanding of all. Credible appointment systems need to contain an essential element of trust. That trust is both in the process and in the common understanding that those given the responsibility to make appointments are committed to applying the criteria which will adjust and gradually transform the exercise of *episkope*.

Can leaders reform structures and systems?

No one would take a top job if they did not think they could make a difference. It would be an ultimately frustrating thing for any leader to think that they could not bring about some measure of change in taking on further responsibility. Why take a job which makes great demands on a person and their family if nothing can be achieved? Understanding the nature of responsibility in a church and the appropriate places where leadership can be given lies at the heart of this exploration. The argument with its conclusions here is that sensitively understood *episkope* or oversight gives the best possible data for strategic interventions and jointly negotiated initiatives. How change is brought about has become a significant theme in this book. We have seen that churches are very good at gradual change. All change has to begin somewhere. Change in understandings of *episkope* could be forced by congregations refusing allegiance to those appointed and inducted into a system to which they cannot give their consent. Alternatively, change can come in as theologians continue to press the significance of agreements made through ecumenical dialogue. Ultimately, permanent and lasting change can be brought in most effectively by those in authority making a conscious decision to develop or adapt their understandings of *episkope* in different ways.

One serious question remains: who oversees the leaders? Since peer accountability, or even collegiality, has yet to become the norm, what checks and balances can be brought to bear on inappropriate leadership. How can there be established some objective control of over-zealous or of inadequate senior leaders? What is needed, especially in episcopal churches where a relationship to the state is being or has been ended, is some form of disciplinary procedure. This has to be objective and not administered by bishops for one another. Again, the credibility of a grievances procedure against senior leaders needs to be established and tested. It should never be easy to remove an inappropriately placed senior leader, but it should be possible.

An example from modern history can show that the state is not always a hindrance and can on occasion see things which a church cannot see about itself. In 1901 the British Prime Minister, Lord Salisbury, was aware that leadership in the church was moving away from the bishops to what he felt were other party power groups.

Here he was exercising his particular form of oversight in relation to an established church. He observed that Charles Gore was an influential public figure in the nation and in the church. Although Gore was associated with the High Church party in the Church of England, Salisbury proposed that he be offered the bishopric of Worcester. It was a controversial appointment but a perceptive one, designed to redress a leadership imbalance. The first thing Gore did on his acceptance was to resign his membership from all church associations and party groupings saying: 'I am sure that a bishop had better own no allegiance to voluntary religious associations which have to take a line on controversial matters of which he may be called to act (within limits) as judge.'[4] When the external control of the state is removed from a church, another external system will, in my view, be needed to call senior leaders in some way to account.

Charles Gore is significant for another reason in our review of how senior office is held. In a perceptive and far-sighted way, Gore saw an episcopal office as having the great potential for oversight of all the people of God in an area, of whatever theological persuasion. He saw that a bishop determined to oversee a whole community can influence public affairs and lead a church in such a way that it wants to address the great community issues of its day. He saw also that a bishop as leader can be a person for a particular time. He was sensitive as to when that time was past, and was one of the few bishops of his day willing to move from one sphere of responsibility to another.

Gore's example can allow us to say that episcopal office in a particular place need not be held until retirement beckons. One of the great aspects of appointment at the peak of performance is that in maturity the experience gained can be used in a final piece of work. The work and its essential concept can be continued in other places, with the order and sense of continuity within the historic episcopate retained, after the particular episcopal title has been resigned.

Can leaders reform structures and systems? Because they 'see-over' a wide range of activity they can, or should, be able to read the signs of the times and see where reform is needed. Ultimately, it is the leaders who legitimize change, working collegially and using the processes of modern synodical debate. Those who become leaders learn their skills through a passion for the gospel and in activities which will have already contributed ideas and reform to their churches. When they become senior leaders they have the same responsibility to continue innovation and reform, but in ways that will bring differing groups together to mobilize and then to consolidate well-negotiated and lasting change.

What would build a culture of trust?

Would all the ingredients described as answers to the questions above bring a renewed atmosphere of trust to our episcopal churches? It is my belief that the starting place has to be with those who do the creative thinking about what *episkope* is and what it should look like in the life of our churches. This needs to be followed by training and preparation systems that will form and shape those who will share in episcopal leadership in the next generations.

The first step towards building a culture of trust is for existing bishops and their staff to be enabled and motivated by new ways of interpreting their office and their responsibilities. The ecumenical documents described in other parts of this book all point to *episkope* as a shared concept. All decisions of a major kind need to be taken by bishops together. This can only be done if bishops can recognize and accept one another's ministries. Bishops are also part of a synodical system and it is here that debate takes place and where resources can be allocated to make sure policies are carried out. When these recognitions are honoured, trust begins to be built.

The second trust-building step is for the wider family membership of episcopal churches to be felt at parish and diocesan level. This is not a plea for episcopalian exclusiveness; quite the reverse. Much more helpful in the context of a plea for the rebuilding of trust is to develop church members who can establish or see a greater understanding of the connectedness of the many and various elements in the make-up of an international community. This is joined-up thinking or, more importantly, thinking that can join up or see the connections between the different parts of a church. It is what takes believers on from membership of a local congregation with all its supportiveness to a bigger concept of an episcopally-based family and ultimately on to the comfort and responsibility of being a member of the Body of Christ.

Regaining our episcopal identity

The culture of episcopal churches is enshrined in a belief that they are united in a common core understanding. When rediscovered in a creative way we see that we share an organized and structured responsibility for one another. In order for this shared understanding to be most effective in the worldwide Christian community, it has to be exercised through a kind of oversight accepted and developed in co-operation with those who are overseen. Without the mutual consent that oversight offered in this way is the best possible system, there can only be distance, fragmentation, divided loyalty and an absence of trust. With it there can be shared responsibility, mutual recognition and a church that draws its life and energy from those who truly believe that this is a good way to care for one another.

Hope rests in the rediscovery of our cultural identity, what it is that forms our essential DNA. This means the rediscovery – or the discovery for the first time for some – of what it means to belong to an episcopal church. We do not belong because we believe solely in priestly ministry, in eucharistically based liturgy, in bishops as leaders in mission or a hundred and one other manifestations of church. We are members of episcopal churches because *episkope* is the one characteristic that binds us together and provides our one unifying concept. Renewed episcopal churches need to be built on a foundation of shared oversight.

No-one will dispute that the need for evangelism is essential and that it is a mission imperative shared by bishop, clergy and laity. Episcopal churches allow a broad base to be brought to this task through the wide range of backgrounds and cultures from which their leadership is drawn. Even more than this, allegiance will only be gained in any organization if it conveys a sense that it is going somewhere. Members will not join and regular adherents will not stay with a denomination, diocese or congregation which lacks a sense of direction. As a consequence clergy and their leaders with broad concepts of oversight will be much more able to read the international signs of the times. They will be able to bring in mission resources from many different countries and cultures. Those being prepared for leadership will have been trained both to energize and to direct from the broadest possible local base. Those choosing a next generation of leaders will have very clear images of *episkope* to inform and guide them about selection criteria.

Episkope cannot become a living reality at the heart of a denomination unless clergy feel that they are an integral part of this shared work. Immediately alongside this, a commitment is required from all members to allow some to be called out to fulfil particular roles and functions and then to support them in their calling. Among these callings, and key to episcopal identity, is that some are called to be deacons, some priests and some bishops. They are called out for specific purposes and to fill some quite specific roles in the church and in their wider communities. This calling and responsibility does not make them into different people, though the temptation is there. They are set apart and given very privileged positions of trust and authority within a continuing shared responsibility for oversight. These positions are only made valid through a wide understanding by many of how their church works and if those appointed have the confidence of the membership that they will continue with a commitment to the shared task. For those appointed there can be a rich and full life filled with privileged opportunities.

Notes

1 Macquarrie, John, *Principles of Christian Theology*, SCM, 1966, Preface, p. vii.
2 Op.cit. pp. 374–91.
3 Op.cit. pp. 246–7.
4 Prestige, G.L., *The life of Charles Gore: a great Englishman*. William Heineman Ltd., 1935. p. 229.

APPENDICES

I

Appointments systems in the Church of England

When a diocese becomes vacant either by the resignation or death of its bishop or through translation to another diocese, a sophisticated and now well publicized process to select another diocesan bishop begins. Once a vacancy is announced two processes begin. The diocese concerned has a Vacancy in See Committee which has ex officio and elected members. It consults widely within the vacant diocese and produces a report. The body that will make the recommendation about an appointment is called the Crown Appointments Commission. It was created in 1997 and has fourteen voting members and two non-voting members.[1] Each member of the Commission may submit names for consideration. The Crown Appointments Secretary and the Archbishops' Secretary for Appointments visit a diocese and produce a profile after wide local consultation. The Diocesan Vacancy in See Committee also produces a profile including a Statement of Needs. These two reports are combined to provide information and guidance when the confidential meetings of the Crown Appointments Commission take place.

The joint profile is presented by the Secretaries at a meeting where confidential information about candidates is matched with evidence in the profile of the diocese. Names for consideration can come both from those elected or appointed by the diocese and from the Archbishops' and Crown Appointments Secretaries. From 2008 the Crown has reduced its influence and there is no longer a full-time appointments Secretary. At the conclusion of its meeting, the Crown Appointments Commission produces two names for the Archbishop of Canterbury or York, depending on the Province of the vacant diocese, to present to the Prime Minister. The Prime Minister chooses from the two names; the convention is that the first name is chosen, and the Crown nominates. It is likely that from the end of 2010 an interviewing process will be established for short-listed candidates for a vacant diocesan see. This is a continuation of the gradual process of making appointments systems more open. In a similar way, advertisements are now placed in the national press inviting names for consideration.

Quite a different process exists for the appointment of suffragan bishops. The choice of a suffragan bishop can be made by the diocesan bishop according to the Suffragan Bishops Act of 1534. Today the choice is still made by the diocesan bishop alone, though he must consult his diocese in drawing up a profile for the appointment. In 1995 a Senior Church Appointments Code of Practice was agreed by the House of Bishops so that the diocesan bishop also consults the Archbishop of the Province, and two names, with the first as priority, are submitted to the Crown with the Archbishop's concurrence. Names can be taken from the Senior Appointments List and the Archbishops' Secretary for Appointments can be consulted about suitable candidates. It is equally open to the diocesan bishop to consider and recommend names of his own choice from those who may not be on the list but who he considers to be particularly suitable. The Church of England is currently engaged in a long debate about the nature and the number of suffragan bishops. A section in Chapter IV discusses the appropriateness of suffragan bishops, and the theology of more than one bishop in a diocese.

Archdeacons are appointed by diocesan bishops, except that when an archdeacon becomes a diocesan bishop his successor is appointed by the Crown. Thus in practice the Crown has for many years had a purely formal role in the appointment of suffragan bishops and practically no role in the appointment of archdeacons.

Cathedral deans are appointed by two processes. The Crown appoints 28 deans to the cathedrals founded before 1882, plus the Deans of Liverpool and Guildford which were new cathedrals and not former parish churches. In the remaining fourteen cathedrals, twelve deans are appointed by the diocesan bishop and two, Sheffield and Bradford, by the Simeon's Trustees. Appointments by the Crown are likely to be made from candidates on the Crown Appointments List and others either by advertisement or by short-listing and interview.[2] Similarly, the Crown plays no part in appointing the great majority of residentiary canons in cathedrals (about 130 out of about 160), or the Dean of Gibraltar. Most of these appointments are also made by the diocesan bishop in consultation with the diocese.

1   The voting members are the two archbishops, three members of the General Synod and three from the House of Laity (elected by their Houses meeting separately), and six members of the vacancy in See Committee of the vacant diocese. The two non-voting members are the Archbishops' Secretary for Appointments and the Prime Minister's Secretary for Appointments. (Recent agreements have reduced the influence of the Prime Minister and his Secretary in this process.)

2   As with almost all matters in the Church of England, there are different practices created by history, custom, statute and local variation.

II

Appointments systems in the Roman Catholic Church

In the Code of Canon Law of the Western Catholic Church published in 1983, it is Canon 377 which sets out the method of appointing bishops. It says 'The Supreme Pontiff freely appoints bishops or confirms those lawfully elected.' (Section § 1) The slightly unusual circumstances, which are a formality in Anglican appointments, is that the cathedral chapters of a number of dioceses in Germany, Austria and Switzerland retain the right to elect their bishop from a list of three names presented to them by the Pope. In every other appointment the choice is made personally by the Pope. Every three years bishops of an Episcopal Conference of bishops can submit names to the Apostolic See.

A two-strand process of consultation takes place to identify names of candidates who might be considered for appointment. The Nuncio will make wide-ranging enquiries through the Diocesan Administrator. These will include a sealed letter with questions to a list of influential and committed practising Catholics including some clergy of the diocese. Reception of the letter, its contents and the replies given are considered to be confidential.

In a similar but less structured process, interested parties are invited to write to the Nuncio describing the needs of the diocese. From this process of consultation a profile of the diocese is constructed to set alongside possible names for appointment. In addition to diocesan consultation, the Nuncio will canvass opinion from other diocesan bishops. In the consideration of names, bishops in other dioceses and Abbots may be brought into the list, and in fact anyone with a legitimate interest.

At the end of this process, which takes approximately six months, the Nuncio will consult and compile a full biography of principal candidates. The complete files are then sent to the office of the Congregation of Bishops in Rome. This full list is accompanied by a *terna*, which is the list of three most recommended names. In the Vatican there is a special office which considers episcopal and other appointments across the world. At this stage it is possible for other existing bishops to contribute an opinion. At the end of this process names will go to the Pope for consideration. He will accept one of the names or refer them back for further consideration. It appears to be the present practice that Pope Benedict XVI takes some time to come to a decision and that he likes there to be a good length of time between one diocesan bishop and the next to ensure an appropriate process of grieving and separation between the retirement or death of one bishop and the arrival of his successor. Once a candidate is identified the Nuncio will make contact with the candidate, who can accept or refuse the appointment.

In many dioceses an Auxiliary Bishop is appointed. This is usually where a diocese is large or if there is some other significant reason why the diocesan bishop needs episcopal assistance to carry out his duties. Auxiliary bishops assist the diocesan in his work. Such an appointment process may narrow the list of those to be considered in the same way that the list of those considered for Anglican diocesan appointments is biased towards those who are already suffragan bishops.

III

Appointments systems in the Methodist Church

For the appointment of a Chairman of District a name is identified by a nomination committee. This is made up of the President of the Methodist Conference and five members from outside the District, appointed by the Methodist Conference and nine members from the District concerned. The District Policy Committee prepares a Statement of Needs and a profile of the kind of person required.

The vacancy is advertised. Ministers can apply themselves, or names can be suggested by others, including from the membership of the nomination committee. The nomination committee will consider all the applications and names put forward. At the end of this process, a nomination, supported by a 'reasoned statement', is put to the District Policy Committee. If accepted, the nomination goes to the District Synod. Any four members of the Synod may propose another name, with a reasoned statement. The Synod votes by ballot on the names presented to it. The names then go forward to the annual meeting of the Methodist Conference as nominations. Any member of the Conference can add a further nomination. If there is more than one candidate the Conference votes by ballot with a simple majority required. In the following year, the Secretary of the Conference proposes that the appointment is confirmed. If this is approved the newly appointed Chair takes up their position having 'shadowed' the outgoing Chair for up to a year. The post is held for a set number of years and can be extended.

BIBLIOGRAPHY

Church of England Reports (in date order)

Partners in Ministry, Chair W. Fenton Morley, Church Information Office CA1640, 1967.

Bishops and Dioceses, ACCM, Report of the ministry working party on the episcopate, 1971.

A Strategy for the Church's Ministry, Chair John Tiller, Church Information Office, 1983.

Deacons in the Ministry of the Church, A Report to the Church of England House of Bishops, 1988. Church House Publishing, GS 802.

Episcopal Ministry: the Report of the Archbishops' Group on the Episcopate, Chair, Chancellor Sheila Cameron, Church House Publishing, London, 1990.

House of Bishops Occasional Paper: Apostolicity and Succession. GS Misc. 432. General Synod of the Church of England, London, 1994.

Working as One Body, The report of the Archbishops' Commission on the organization of the Church of England, Chair Michael Turnbull, Church House Publishing, 1995.

Bishops in Communion: Collegiality in the service of the koinonia of the Church, GS Misc. 580, House of Bishops Occasional Paper, Church House Publishing, 2000.

Working with the Spirit: choosing diocesan bishops. A review of the Crown Appointments Commission and related matters, GS1405, Church House Publishing, 2001.

Resourcing Bishops: The first report of the Archbishops' Review Group on bishops' needs and resources. Church House Publishing, 2001.

Resourcing Archbishops: The second report of the Archbishops' Review Group on bishops' needs and resources. Church House Publishing, 2002.

Suffragan Bishops: GS Misc. &33. Church House Publishing, 2004.

Women Bishops in the Church of England, A report of the House of Bishops' working party on women in the episcopate, Church House Publishing, 2004.

Talent and Calling: a review of the law and practice regarding the appointments to the offices of suffragan bishop, dean, archdeacon and residentiary canon. The report of a working party chaired by Sir Joseph Pilling, Archbishops' Council, 2007.

From Frustration to Fulfilment, the final 10 years of licensed ministry, Senior Clergy Group, Chair John Lee. Archbishops' Council of the C of E, 2007.

Ecumenical Reports

Report of the Anglican-Methodist Unity Commission: London SPCK and The Epworth Press, 1968.

Baptism, Eucharist and Ministry, World Council of Churches, Faith and Order Paper No 111. 1982.

The Porvoo Common Statement, Council for Christian Unity of the Church of England, Occasional Paper No. 3. 1993.

Catechism of the Catholic Church, Geoffrey Chapman, 1994.

The Sign We Give, A report from the Working party on Collaborative Ministry for the Bishops Conference of England and Wales, 1995.

Called to be One. CTE Publications, 1996.

The Report of the Meissen Commission 1991–6, Church House Publishing GS Misc, 1997.

The Reully Common Statement, Church House Publishing GS Misc 566, 1997.

Carta Oecumenica, Conference of European Churches and the Roman Catholic Council of European Bishops, Church House Publishing, GS Misc 713, 2003.

The Nature of Oversight: Leadership, Management and Governance in the Methodist Church in Great Britain and *What is a District Chair?* Minutes of Conference 2005.

Biographies and autobiographies

Carey, George, *Know the Truth: A Memoir*, Harper Perennial, 2005.

Charles, William (ed.), *Basil Hume: Ten Years On*, Burns & Oates/ Continuum 2009.

Du Boulay, Shirley, *Tutu: voice of the voiceless*, Hodder & Stoughton, 1988.

Hewitt, Gordon (ed.) *Strategist for the Spirit, Leslie Hunter, Bishop of Sheffield 1939–62*. Beckett, 1985

Iremonger, F. A., *William Temple, Archbishop of Canterbury: His Life and Letters*, OUP, 1948.

James, Eric, *Bishop John A. T. Robinson: Scholar, Pastor, Prophet*, Collins, 1987.

Kent, John, *William Temple: Church, State and Society in Britain, 1880–1950*, Cambridge, 1992.

Küng, Hans, *Disputed Truth: Memoirs*, Continuum, London & New York, 2008.

Mantle, Jonathan, *Archbishop: the life and times of Robert Runcie*, Sinclair-Stevenson, 1991.

Moltmann, Jürgen, *A Broad Place: An autobiography*, SCM, London, 2007.

Prestige, G. L., *The life of Charles Gore: a great Englishman*. William Heineman Ltd, 1935.

General bibliography

Adie, Michael, *Held Together: an exploration of coherence*, DLT, 1997.

Arbuckle, Gerald, *Refounding the Church: Dissent for Leadership*, Geoffrey Chapman, 1993.

Banks, Sarah and Gallagher, Ann, *Ethics and Professional Life*, Palgrave MacMillan, 2008.

Becker, Penny E., *Congregations in conflict; cultural models of local religious life*, Cambridge, 1999.

Boyd-MacMillan, E. and Savage, S., *Transforming Conflict*, Foundation for Church Leadership, 2008.

Brown, David, *Releasing Bishops for Relationship*, Foundation for Church Leadership, 2008.

Bultmann, Rudolph, *Theology of the New Testament*, Vol. II, p. 102, Nashville, 1989.

Cameron, Helen, *Resourcing Mission: Practical Theology for Changing Churches*, SCM, 2010.

Cavanagh, Lorraine, *By One Spirit: Reconciliation and renewal in Anglican life*, Peter Lang, 2009.

Cox, Harvey, *The Secular City*, Macmillan, New York, 1966.

Croft, Steven, *Ministry in Three Dimensions*, DLT, 1999.

Davie, Grace, *Religion in Modern Europe: A Memory Mutates*, OUP, 2000.

Davies, Douglas and Guest, Matthew, *Bishops, wives and children; Spiritual capital across the generations*. Ashgate, 2007.

Dickens, A. G., *Reformation and Society in Sixteenth Century Europe*, Thames & Hudson, London, 1966.

Duffy, Eamon, *The Voices of Morebath, Reformation and Rebellion in an English Village*, Yale University Press, 2001.

Dulles, Avery S. J., *Models of the Church*, Gill & Macmillan, Dublin, 1989.

Ecclestone, Giles (ed.), *The Parish Church? Explorations in the relationship of the Church and the World*. Mowbray, 1988.

Finney, John, *Finding Faith Today*, British and Foreign Bible Society, 1992.

Francis Leslie J. and Robbins, Mandy, *Personality and the Practice of Ministry*, Grove Books, Pastoral Series, 2004.

Fraser, Ian, *Reinventing Church: insights from small Christian communities and reflections on a journey among them*. Private Publication, 2003.

Greenwood, Robin, *Parish priests: for the sake of the Kingdom*, SPCK, 2009.

Gregory the Great: *Medieval Sourcebook, The Book of Pastoral Rule*, c. 590.

Grundy, Malcolm, *Understanding Congregations*, Continuum, 1998.

Grundy, Malcolm, *What they don't teach you at Theological College*, Canterbury Press, Norwich, 2003.

Grundy, Malcolm, *What's New in Church Leadership?*, Canterbury Press, Norwich, 2007.

Gutierrez, Gustavo, *We Drink From Our Own Wells*, SCM, 1984.

Haliburton, John, *The Authority of a Bishop*, SPCK, 1987.

Hastings, Adrian, *A History of English Christianity 1920-1985*, Collins, Fount, 1986.

Hebblethwaite, Peter, *The New Inquisition: Schillebeeckx and Küng*, Collins, Fount Paperbacks, 1980.

Higginson, Richard. *Transforming Leadership: A Christian Approach to Management*. SPCK, 1996.

Hobson, Theo, *Milton's Vision: the Birth of Christian Liberty*, Continuum, London, 2008.

Hooker, Richard, *Of the Laws of Ecclesiastical Polity*, Book VII, Clarendon Press, Oxford, 1890.

Howatch, Susan. *Ultimate Prizes*, Collins, London, 1989.

Hull, John, *Mission-Shaped Church: A theological response*, SCM Press, 2006.

Küng, Hans, *On being a Christian*, Collins, Fount Paperbacks, 1978.

Küng, Hans, *Why Priests?*, Collins, Fount paperbacks, 1978.

Longford, Frank. *The Bishops: a study of leaders in the church today* 1986. Sidgwick & Jackson, London.

Macquarrie, John, *Principles of Christian Theology*, SCM, 1966.

Maynard, Theodore, *The Life of Thomas Cranmer*, Staples Press, London, 1956.

Messer, Donald E. *Contemporary Images of Christian Ministry*, Abingdon, Nashville, 1989.

Moltmann, Jürgen *The Church in the Power of the Spirit*, SCM Press, Second Edition, 1992.

Moore, Paul, *The Church Reclaims the City*, SCM, 1965.

Moore, Peter, *Bishops, but what kind?* SPCK, 1982.

Nazir-Ali, Michael, *Shapes of the Church to come*. Kingsway Publications, 2001.

Nelson, John (ed.), *Management and Ministry*, MODEM, Canterbury Press, Norwich, 1996.

Nelson, John (ed.), *Leading, Managing, Ministering*, MODEM, Canterbury Press, Norwich, 1999.

Nelson, John with Adair, John (ed.), *Creative Church Leadership*, Canterbury Press, Norwich, 2004.

Nelson, John (ed.), *How to Become a Creative Church Leader*, Canterbury Press, Norwich, 2008.

Newbigin, Leslie, *The Gospel in a Pluralist Society*, SPCK, 1989.

Niebuhr, H. Richard, *Christ and Culture*, Harper, Torchbooks, New York, 1956.

Österlin, Lars *The Churches of Northern Europe in Profile: a thousand years of Anglo-Nordic relations*, Canterbury Press, Norwich, 1995.

Owen, David, *The Hubris Syndrome: Bush Blair and the Intoxication of Power*, Politicos, Methuen, 2007.

Owen, David, *In Sickness and in Health: illness in heads of government during the last 100 years*, Methuen, 2009.

Platten, S. (ed.) *Anglicanism and the Western Tradition*, Canterbury Press, 2003.

Podmore, Colin, *Aspects of Anglican Identity*, Church House Publishing, 2005.

Ramsey, A. M. *The Gospel and the Catholic Church*, Longmans, London, 1936.

Reed, Bruce, *The Dynamics of Religion, process and movement in Christian churches*, London, DLT, 1978.

Rudge, Peter, *Management in the Church*, McGraw Hill, 1976.

Russell, Anthony, *The Clerical Profession*, SPCK, 1980.

Ryman, Björn (ed.), *Nordic Folk Churches: a contemporary church history*, Eardmans Publishing, Michigan/Cambridge, 2005.

Savage, Sara and Boyd-MacMillan, Eolene, *The Human Face of Church*, Canterbury Press, Norwich, 2007.

Schillebeeckx, Edward, *Ministry: a case for change*, SCM, London, 1985.

Schillebeeckx, Edward, *The Church with a Human Face*, SCM, London, 1985.

Sheppard, David and Warlock, Derek, *Better Together*, Hodder & Stoughton, 1988.

Simpson, John, *Mad World My Masters*, Pan Macmillan, 2001,

Sørensen, Eva and Torfing, Jacob (ed.), *Theories of Democratic Network Governance*, Palgrave MacMillan, 2008.

Sykes, Stephen, *The Integrity of Anglicanism*, Mowbray, London, 1978.

Tillich, Paul, *Systematic Theology*, vol. 2. James Nisbett & Co, 1964. Clark, Edinburgh, 1999.

Torrance, Thomas F., *Royal Priesthood: A theology of Ordained Ministry*. T & T, 1993.

Warren, Robert, *Building Missionary Congregations*, Board of Mission Occasional Paper no. 4, Church House Publishing, 1995.

Warren, Robert, *Signs of life: How goes the Decade of Evangelism?* Church House Publishing, 1996.

Watts, Frazer, Nye, Rebecca, and Savage, Sara, *Psychology for Christian Ministry*, Routledge, 2002.

Wickham, E. R. *Church and People in an Industrial City*, Lutterworth, 1957.

INDEX